THE LAST HUNDRED

THE LAST HUNDRED
Munros, Beards and a Dog

HAMISH BROWN

MAINSTREAM
PUBLISHING

EDINBURGH AND LONDON

First published in Great Britain in 1994 by
MAINSTREAM PUBLISHING COMPANY (EDINBURGH) LTD
7 Albany Street
Edinburgh EH1 3UG

Reprinted 1996

ISBN 1 85158 607 5

A catalogue record for this book is available from the British Library

Typeset in 11/12½ Cheltenham by Intype, London
Printed in Hong Kong by H&Y Printing Ltd

Contents

Introduction 7

MUNROITIS 11
    An Incurable Disease 13
    The Game of Listing Hills 18
    Camp by the Buachaille 24

MANY A MUNRO 27
    Christmas Peaks (Beinn a' Ghlo) 28
    Music 32
    The Huge Concept of Beinn Dorain 33
    Under Ben Alder 39
    A Hundred Years Ago 41
    Squelching Across Scotland 45
    Lessons from Experience 49
    Crossing the Moor 56

BRAEHEAD, THE STORY OF A SCHOOL 57
    Snowed-in at Glendoll 77
    A Remembered Traverse of the Cuillin Ridge 79
    The Wanting 86

AND MORE MUNROS 87
    All About Attow 88
    Glen Pean Cottage 92
    Mull: Easter on the Heights 93
    In Search of a Maiden 101
    Wyvis – Hill of Terror 106
    Beginnings 110

STORM – THE STORY OF A DOG 111
    Storm's Last Munro 137

ONE GAME, MANY APPROACHES 145
    The Ben Nevis Observatory 146
    The Harlot 149
    The First Munro on Skis 150
    Last Run: Coire na Ciste 156
    The World of the Red Deer 157

In the Rut   163
The Menace of Midges   165

LASTLY   169
  Over the Top   170
  Protected Out of Our Own   174
  Scotland – the Rot   179
  Pity Poor Foinaven   183
    Closing the Book   186
  Schiehallion! Schiehallion! Schiehallion!   187

Introduction

I am not a Munro-bagger. I keep having to say this. Admittedly I've climbed many Munros, possibly far too many, but this was fortuitous, a lucky chance if you like, and Munros never were, and most certainly aren't, the be all and end all of my hill interests. It is a strange British trait to take pastimes so very seriously (and treat serious issues as a big joke) and I wince when encountering youths who declare themselves fervent Munro-ists and then give their 'tally' of, say, 12 Munros. Come hell or high water (and the Scottish hills are good at combining the two) they are out every weekend, every holiday, just to gain another tick on the list. Thank God for Muriel then and her mockery and mickey-taking. The message is still there. Extremists, fundamentalists, are dangerous. Munros are for fun.

The title of this book may be taking the mickey out of *The First Fifty* but it agrees with the joys and pleasures garnered. I'm no Oor Wullie look-alike in puking colours and the Grey and the Brown would probably agree to differ on a whole range of topics. We'd *enjoy* arguing though (something of a national trait) but, name any Munro, and we could talk the hours away together. The Munros are a great, shared blessing. Our books are basically Munro gossip. As this could just be my last such, the title is perhaps apposite (I'm not quitting Munros, I want to write more on other topics, that's all), and I'll take the chance to let off steam on various matters. Far too often now Munro-bagging is Munro-mugging. How and why it is done I think *is* important. There is an arrogance of approach today, which I find deeply disturbing. Instant-Munroing is as unsavoury (and indigestible) as instant food. The hills must be loved, for themselves, and not just for quick self-gratification. In other spheres that is defined as rape.

My most active Munro years were the dozen I spent taking Fife youngsters into the wilds. As far as I know, mine was the first appointment in a state school to do what has become outdoor education and we roamed Scotland to the extent that, eventually, pupils from Braehead School had climbed every Munro. Munro-bagging was a lively part of their world. What has happened in the last decade to outdoor education (like any other education) is a sorry story but then I believe we largely get what we deserve from our elected representatives.

In those years, taking beardless school parties away constantly led to the repetitive problem of shaving off my stubble every time I returned so, in self-defence, I simply grew a beard, which has remained, thereby gaining several more days in life for more pleasurable activities (I've aye grudged the hours spent on servicing this poor human machine).

One of my great delights has been the companionship of two dogs, the

Shetland collies, Kitchy and Storm. The first I inherited when my father died and he, after a traumatic start, became the hill mascot of the Braehead kids. Storm chose me but, like Kitchy, did all the Munros so they have their part in my backward look over the mountains. I am un-apologetic about telling so much about Storm. He was the best companion with whom I did most Munros: always enthusiastic, uncomplaining, tireless, good-tempered. I wish all my friends were like him. I wish I was!

This may appear a bit of a rag-bag of a book, full of started topical hares, comments, judgments, some repetitions, sometimes loquacious, sometimes spartan, whiles cheery, whiles dour. But that is how it is, in life with the Munros, as any other. How dull life would be otherwise. It is *because* life is so dull otherwise, and for so many, that such numbers are now breaking out and heading for the hills. I did it myself, as I tell in that first-ever book about the Munros, *Hamish's Mountain Walk*, and I've kept right on doing it. A systematic Munro coverage would be both boring and impractical. Some hill days are more memorable than others, just as some hills are finer than others (who'd swap any Geal Charn – or all of them – for one An Teallach?), and so this book has to be inconsistent and selective. I'm often enough accused of shit-stirring but, with hindsight, I've often been right in so doing. Blowing the whistle. This may be my last opportunity to do so. My despair at Britain, at Scotland, is too deep now. I want sunnier, unspoilt mountains and warmer, hopeful peoples.

I am the complete pessimist at heart which means I'm constantly 'surprised by joy' (the optimist, perforce, is constantly being disappointed), and plenty of the best days of my life have ambushed me on the Munros – so I write about Munros. The *last* hundred? I doubt it.

Misunderstandings could arise from glancing at any part of this book so please reserve judgment till the end. When wrong sticks are picked up they can still give painful beatings. Reminds me of the story of the shepherd and his girlfriend who were watching the spectacle of the tups (rams) being put to the ewes. Eventually he leered at his girl, 'I could be doing that myself,' to which he received the deserved reply 'Ah well, dear, that's no problem. There's plenty of ewes in the next field too.'

I've included odd poems which have Munro connections. Some of these have appeared elsewhere but, despite public interest, editors are loathe to use such – or hill fiction – and most article contributors seldom quote or produce much in the way of novelty. The late twentieth century faces a new illiteracy alas and cannot digest anything longer than a television 'bite'.

As a practical help the pieces describing specific Munros or groups have the Ordnance Survey Landranger map sheet number given after the titles (coded as OSLR 20 for instance). People often find reading such descriptions with the relevant maps available makes for greater clarity.

Many of the pieces used here first appeared, in some form, in magazines or newspapers and their re-creation is gratefully acknowledged. I apologise for odd repetitions that unavoidably crop up as a result of such recycling – but their reuse may have saved one tree from being pulped! My thanks to the following (some of which have also been recycled): *The Alpine*

Sgurr nan Clach Geala in the Fannich Forest

Journal, The Angry Corrie, Canoe Camper, The Challenger, Climber and Hill-walker, Country Life, The Courier, Footloose, The Herald, The Great Outdoors, The Lady, The Scots Magazine, The Scotsman, Scottish Field, A Scottish Child-hood, Scottish Mountaineering Club Journal, Skier, and *Sunday Standard.*

Hamish Brown
Kinghorn, 1994

On Beinn Sgritheall above Glenelg, when Hogmanays had snow

MUNROITIS

1891 saw the publication of the original Munro's Tables *in the first volume of the Scottish Mountaineering Club's* Journal, *so not surprisingly the centenary brought forth a flutter of articles commemorating this regrettable or celebratory event. 'An Incurable Disease' was written for* The Great Outdoors *then. 'The Game of Listing Hills' I hope will cause complaints and personal compilations. The other pieces were written at various times and are included to show my own Munro genesis and how very little we change in attitudes over a lifetime.*

I'm certainly not a wining-and-dining type but 1991 gave one event which was greatly enjoyed: the Munros Centenary Dinner in Edinburgh. Had I not been asked to 'perform' ('show a few slides of Munros') I might well have missed a friendly, happy evening with an extraordinary diversity of people, all linked by this quixotic pastime. Roll on 2001, which seems the next logical date to celebrate. Only, where on earth will we gather for the numbers involved? Murrayfield perhaps (for soccer may still await its comparable international ground) or even the top of the Ben?

See you there.

Lord Berkley's Seat from Sgurr Fiona (An Teallach)

An Incurable Disease

Over the years I've climbed quite a few Munros. And why? For the only valid reason. For fun. I also believe it should be fun at the time and not just in retrospect, and there are very few moments when I've felt a wish to be somewhere else, doing something else. Agony is quite often part of ecstasy and accepted as such. An element of challenge is essential to human well-being. We were a leaner, fitter race in the austerity of wartime rationing than we are now with the flabby self-indulgence of prosperity. It is not only in diet that we need roughage!

Munro-bagging has become very much one of the games outdoor types play and some of the blame for this popularity is laid at my door. This makes me smile a somewhat wry smile for I have never been a Munro-bagger in the way thousands seem to be today. The great outdoors was simply my happy escape, from before my teens even.

As a war refugee in South Africa I roamed alone into the Valley of the Thousand Hills, made friends locally (not knowing anything of apartheid) and learnt the basics of self-sufficiency. Scotland after that was simply widening horizons. Once I could out-walk, out-cycle my parents I'd go off and spend whole holidays in the Highlands. Ben Nevis, alone, in my early teens was my first Munro – I had to deal with cloud and rain and watched the water in my anorak pockets turn to ice.

We humans are natural survivors on the whole. When we are frightened by circumstances we back down. Experience is the sum of near misses. I did not know Ben Nevis was a Munro any more than I knew the cliffs of Lochnagar offered climbing – until a climber gave me a wigging for climbing up those cliffs by myself, in plimsolls, and quite happily too. I was simply pushing out the circles of experience. What I find sad now is that many people never push themselves, and rest content with a low level of performance – and reward.

As the jingle says:

> Life itself can't give you joy
> Unless you really will it,
> Life just gives you time and space,
> It's up to you to fill it.

I'd accepted wildlife, especially birds and flowers, as part of the natural order. I loved the history and lore of the Highlands and I read voraciously. It was a very greedy grasping of our inheritance which made me very much an all-rounder. I did some Munros but I also did some climbing, skiing, canoeing, sailing, island-bagging, foreign travelling, botanising, bird-watching and so on. *Being there* was what mattered, not any artificial demarcating or labelling. It was the land I loved, so the dust of it went through the pores of my soul; which is why conservation plays a large part in my life now, for I have seen the death of so many beautiful places over the years.

This is my background then. My deeds and thoughts have remained constant, my attitudes largely unchanged. There have been periods when one or other pastime has dominated, as it has to do to satisfy the desire for deeper knowledge or improved performance. Even before doing all the Munros in a single trip I'd stated these beliefs, and said I'd not be heart-broken if circumstances dictated I'd never climb another Munro. I could then look at more Pictish symbol stones or enjoy larger hours gardening. I could happily fill half a dozen lives! Sixteen years passed before I completed the Munros. Now they are done by people who haven't even reached that number of years.

Only in the last four years of those 16 was I quite consciously pushing Munros. They were teaching years, and Munros became something eager youngsters could enjoy – so we did plenty. The school completed its Munros, my two dogs completed their Munros, I completed the Munros a couple more times, creating solo, summer and winter tallies.

The years of teaching ended and two years of discontent followed. The Munros were my escape from that. And there was the great challenge to do them all in a single, self-propelled walk. It became a self-fulfilled dream and one of life's real highs, which nothing can take away. I wrote a book about it – the first-ever book about Munros – and this just hit the time when 'feet' disappeared from our maps and Munros were in a state of atrophy. How thoroughly British, that an antique, obsolete measurement is now our yardstick of ambition.

Hamish's Mountain Walk, so long in print, points to the popularity of the Munros. Books are far more likely to meet a demand than create a new one. To the non-hillgoer a book on Munros would be as attractive as a book on jungle horticulture to an Eskimo! The book on the Munros didn't grab non-hillgoers, it caught the eye of the already rapidly expanding number of people involved with hills and gave them an interesting theme, a useful goal, and a bit of inspiration.

People like having a target and they like ticking lists. Munro-ing may be no worse than stamp collecting but, of course, we believe it to be far far better, giving regular healthy exercise and a knowledge of the Highlands gained in the best possible way.

Any pastime will acquire a lunatic fringe. So what? At least the game is now out in the open. I can recall the days when Munro-bagging was regarded as slightly *infra dig*, the *Munro's Tables* were wrapped in brown paper and studied in the tent by candlelight once everyone else was asleep.

Only eight people had climbed the Munros before the Second World War. The Rev. A. E. Robertson, the inimitable first, in 1901. Another Reverend, A. R. G. Burn, was second – in 1923. He also added the subsidiary Tops. Five years later J. A. Parker added the 'Furth of Scotland' (the English,

Welsh and Irish 'Munros'). It has always struck me that this sort of grand slam should be the objective. Taking the Munros-only option is a mere pass; adding Tops and Furth is the honours. When people say to me they've done the Munros I immediately ask 'And Tops?' – or the job's only poorly done.

J. R. Corbett was Munroist No. 4 and he not only did the Tops but climbed all the 2,000-ft summits and bequeathed to us his list of now eponymous 2,500-ft summits; the post-graduate course for many Munroists and one I'd recommend doing simultaneously rather than afterwards. People find Corbetts are astonishingly good value and they are often quite as demanding and enjoy an even greater geographical spread. They are good bait for the anti-Munroist!

Of the four other pre-war Munroists two are still alive, so the game must be good for you! After the war the game was resumed. In 1964 Philip Tranter completed the first-ever second round. About 25 people have done so now and several have done subsequent rounds to that. I would question the motivation of any Munroist who has done the Munros and is *not* ticking off a repeat round. There is certainly an element, alas, where list-ticking is the end of the exercise instead of the means to the never-ending end of just being there in the wilds. Anyone of normal vigour should still be Munro-ing or the derogatory epithets are deserved. The multiple-Munroists are simply out on the hill a lot: they are not desperately ticking Munros.

Of the first 30 Munroists 20 were Scottish Mountaineering Club members, but this monopoly has long since been broken. The *SMC Journal* still produces its annual list of those who have completed Munros, Tops, Furth, etc., but there must be hundreds now who are not so listed for the numbers involved have escalated enormously. I came in as No. 62 in 1965. The 100-up came in 1971, the 500 in 1987. Now it is away past 1,000.

There have been several husband-and-wife teams and all manner of generation-links from father-son to parents and children. The wife of No. 6 (1938) joined him as No. 469 in 1986! To date 'fastest' or 'youngest' has not become a lure but there are signs of this changing. When I did the Munros as a continuous trip the press (not the climbing/walking press) latched on to the 112 days of this as 'the fastest-ever' – a label which was anathema to me, so when, in 1985, Martin Moran did them in his 83-day winter haul, I was quite relieved. In 1988 Mark Elsegood ran the Munros in 66 days with car assistance, which let Martin off the hook as well.

A bit of me is curious, of course, about just how fast they could be done, with or without vehicular assistance. In 1990 the fell-runner Hugh Symonds ran all the Munros, plus English and Welsh and Irish 3,000-footers in 100 days, without using transport. Ian Leighton (No. 512) has made some extraordinary runs already, such as coast-to-coast in five days over 50 Munros, and now the next objective is all the Munros in 50 days. As I write the 'record' stands at 52 days (Johnston and Gibson). The permutations are endless. A few summers ago a touch of the lunatic fringe came in with a mountain-bike attempt at the Munros. And I thought taking my dogs up the Inaccessible Pinnacle was a bit daft!

Most people treat Munro-bagging as a light-hearted pastime. Its vagaries can infuriate but unlike the Corbetts, which have a strict mathematical definition, the Munros have a purely subjective definition. The last major revisions were forced by the new heights from the Ordnance Survey. These appeared not long before the maps went metric so, in some cases, they were not even noticed by walkers.

Revision is a much more complex business than the angry letter-writers realise. I remember the howls when Sgurr nan Ceannaichean, above Achna-shellach, was promoted and all the lazy louts who had just bagged Moruisg had to return for Ceannaichean. If they had made the obvious, classic traverse of Moruisg they would have already been over Ceannaichean and received a bonus not a tax reminder.

Parting thoughts on Munroitis, passing the centenary of the *Tables*? 'Take it easy' would sum up my feelings. Let the racers race – and nod, if you cannot bow, in their direction. (Because only one person holds a world sprint record does not mean everyone else is jealous, moans or gives up running.) The hills have had a strong element of tolerance and I'd hate to see this lost. 'Tread softly.' The sheer numbers involved are creating pressures on a fairly fragile landscape. Remedial work may not be beautiful but may be unavoidable. Litter really gets my goat and Munroists-a-plenty sin in this matter.

'Take your time.' There is no additional merit in having climbed all the Munros at 22 rather than 32 or 42 or any other age. There is a far richer reward in just going to the Highlands and taking them for themselves, exploring, wandering, enjoying every aspect with the *Tables* kept at home and only ticked periodically.

Climb the Corbetts as well, explore islands, learn about the past, the wildlife; absorb the great outdoors and then, when you suddenly find you've passed 200 Munros, well, get cracking in a last romp of tidying-up. I feel sorry for most people finishing the Munros early in life. So many just fade away. Let's keep the Munros gently on course between the Ayatollahs and the clowns.

After all that I forgot to define a Munro, but I don't think there can be many readers who don't know what a Munro is. The definition I tend to give to the innocent seeker after enlightenment is that a Munro is a parlous natural hazard found on the Scottish hills. It gives rise to the psychological ailment of Munroitis, for which there is no known cure.

Storm with a Corbett and a Munro in the background

The Game of Listing Hills

Here is a list of 50 hills in Scotland. They read like a collection of malts and one could become quite tipsy over them. They are not arranged in any order but were listed more or less as the names were suggested.

The inane games climbers play. But what do you do when marooned in a mountain hut in the Atlas during a 48-hour blizzard, when there are no cards, no pocket chess and the two books have been shredded and passed round? We traversed the hut walls and climbed round the table (a good Extreme) and quickly destroyed any thoughts the continentals had about the 'quiet' British. I reinvented Book Cricket from dim memories of misspent time in Latin classes. We compiled lists of likes and dislikes, of favourite musicians, artists, authors . . . I suppose it had to come round to listing mountains in the end. A Scottish Top Twenty hills? Here are 50, without much thinking. I was made scribe as I could actually spell most of them. Try the taste of speaking them aloud: malts, quite definitely. I've given them in a sort of geographical order, for convenience, not as any indication of progressive merit.

> Morven (Caithness), Foinaven/Arkle, Stac Polly, Cul Mor, Ben More Coigach, Conival/Ben More Assynt, Seana Braigh, Sgurr na Clach Geala, Beinn Dearg Mor, A' Mhaighdean, Slioch, Baosbheinn, Beinn Dearg (Torridon), Fuar Tholl, the Applecross Corbetts, Bidean/Lurg Mor, Beinn Fhada (Attow), Sgurr Fhuaran (Five Sisters), A' Chralaig/Mullach, In. Pin., Alasdair, Am Basteir, The Storr, The Clisham, Askival, Beinn Sgritheall, Sgurr na Ciche, Ben More (Mull), Ben Resipol, Ben Tee, Garbheinn (Ardgour), Starav, Stob Ghabhar, Beinn Dorain, Ben Lui, Ben More/Stob Binnein, Ben Lawers, Beinn a' Ghlo, Ben Vrackie, Vorlich/ Stuc a' Chroin, Ben Lomond, The Cobbler, Goat Fell, Cir Mhor, The Merrick, Paps of Jura, Ben Macdhui, Ben Avon/Beinn a' Bhuird, Cairntoul, Beinn Rhinnes.

Most of the above appeared in somebody or other's list and I suppose they are all Top Twenty material. (When we played this game in a magazine many years ago 80 hills were named altogether.) And no doubt you're thinking 'Where's So and So? . . . Definitely names missing from the list.' Yes, there are 20 names missing from that list. This is a list of the also-rans!

We had heated debate, walk-outs, sulks and a near ice-axe murder before lining up the Top Twenty, roughly in consensus order. Very rough. I wonder what the continentals thought of this noisy paper game that filled the evening?

1. An Teallach. 2. Liathach. 3. Ben Nevis. 4. Buachaille Etive Mor. 5. Lochnagar. 6. Sgurr nan Gillean. 7. Ben Alder. 8. Suilven. 9. Cruachan. 10. Alligin. 11. Bidean. 12. The Saddle. 13. Braeriach. 14. Creag Meagaidh. 15. Ceathreamhnan. 16. Schiehallion. 17. Blaven. 18. Ladhar Bheinn. 19. Beinn Eighe. 20. Aonach Eagach.

If Scotland was nothing else except those 70 hills it would be a mountain richness yet there are over 500 peaks in the Munros and Corbetts lists, quite apart from small hills like Stac Pollaidh or Morven, which happily avoid being height-listed at all. It doesn't do any harm to just sit back and wonder about our wealth now and then. Reminds me of a dreary dinner which the late Philip Tranter and I attended. To take our minds off the long, dull speeches we, periodically, in turn, whispered the name of a hill and went into our respective daydreams as we fished out our memories of days on those hills. You can play alone or in company – quite a good game for dentists' waiting-rooms, supermarket check-out queues or international airports.

After the lists had cooled from the lava flow of their creation we fell to discussing them. What common denominator was there in the Top Twenty? Bigness was an obvious factor. All are Munros and a fair proportion are big Munros, big in altitude and big in their territorial sprawl. They are mostly demanding hills, both from that bigness and because they are well-endowed with cliffs, corries and ridges that offer summer or winter climbing of quality. They are hills for mountaineers. The 20 have probably caused more fiascos and benightments, and killed more people than have the 50. I find this reassuring.

Let me hasten to add it is not the accident statistic that reassures but the fact that the list was obviously a reflection of activity and experience. A gang of ordinary hill enthusiasts knew what was best because they'd been there, up there, in all seasons, doing all manner of things, and producing a list which shows the zest for adventure is very much with us still. That is reassuring.

The 20 are all dominant hills. They look well from most angles. They look well from below. And the views from them are top class. Most shoot into a special category (almost an alpine quality) in winter conditions. To a lesser degree those attributes are held by the 50 as well.

The 50 are more diverse. Many are relatively small but make up for height with the roughness of their terrain. The summit views are all superb. Most are *shapely* hills: brutal and bold (Baosbheinn, Garbh Bhein of Ardgour), symmetrical and graceful (Goat Fell, Sgurr na Ciche), massive and corrie bitten (Macdhui, Applecross). A high proportion have sea views or overlook big lochs as part of their magic. The variety defies any tidy categorising.

Bigness underlies the Top Twenty. Schiehallion apart, they are not hills to be romped over in half a day. Some will take half a day just to reach. Every Munro can be done in a day from a car or a comfortable base but there are some (Ben Alder, Ceathreamhnan) where one is usually glad enough to camp or bothy nearer at hand. (Note how quality tells: Sgurr nan Ceathreamhnan is in the 20, Mam Soul/Carn Eige, close by and bigger, don't even make the 50.)

When you walk Scotland coast-to-coast one quickly noted feature of our hills is the extra height that has to be put in to climb Munros or Corbetts in the west. The starting point is on or little above sea-level. Once the Great Glen is passed, however, and the initial uphill made, eastwards, then that gain is held right through until one descends out of the Cairngorms or the Braes of Angus. The Buachaille, Ben Alder, Braeriach, Schiehallion all give you a thousand feet of free start. One, two, three on the list make you climb every inch of the way. The main Highlands, seen from the stratosphere, appear almost flat, flat and wrinkled, for it is essentially a weathered plateau. Considering it is a weathered plateau the surprise is how fine so many hills can be, in themselves, and that unbelievable forces went into their creation – Liathach is geologically upside down!

Bigness does not necessarily enhance the summit view, sometimes it reduces it. The view from our highest summit, Ben Nevis, I don't consider to be as fine as the view from Suilven which is not even Corbett height. Ben Nevis is too dominating. The view is lost. (There's a feeling of this on top of the Matterhorn. The view lacks the one great eye-catcher – the Matterhorn.) Corbetts, on average, are better viewpoints than Munros because they have a separateness to them. I think there would be more Corbetts in the lists if it were not for Munros being such a fixation that a 'dull' Munro will prove a bigger lure than a superb Corbett. Beinn Dearg (Loch Broom) is a big hill but I'd suggest the neighbouring Corbett, Beinn Eneglair, has the better view.

Sometimes hills crowd themselves. You can't see the scenery for the scenery. Corbetts are seldom so cluttered with other hills, so the views are wider – and the better for this. An Teallach, Ceathreamhnan, Schiehallion are uncluttered so their views are remarkable. The Corbett Beinn a' Chuallaich, above Kinloch Rannoch, is a better viewpoint than Schiehallion because the Matterhorn/Schiehallion is part of the view. Geal Charn, the Corbett north of Loch Arkaig, is a superlative viewpoint and worth all the Munro Geal Charns combined. And how many fail to climb Ben Tee (a mere Corbett) – because they are bagging the Loch Lochy Munros? The lists are very subjective. Fashion dictates quite a bit of our mountain activity, walking or climbing, and there were huge gaps in the knowledge of Scottish hills among the party drawing up the lists.

It would be very difficult to drop any of these hills but obviously many of our *best* views are hardly known: Ben Tee or Geal Charn, as mentioned, Sgurr an Utha above Glenfinnan, Am Bathach above Cluanie, Sgorr na Diollaid (Cannich), Beinn a'Bha' ach Ard (Struy), Beinn Dronaig, Carn na Saobhaidhe . . .

Something else is missing from the lists. There are few peaks on big ridges. Stob Ban of the Mamores was nearby in but, arguably, there are several other Mamores summits as good. Even allowing Carn Mor Dearg to go in with the Ben, there is nothing from the Aonachs – nor from the Lapaichs, Affric, Conbhairean . . . Grey Corries sweep, the Saddle and Sgurr Fhuaran are extremities of ridges, or so much bigger, that they are often

An Teallach from Beinn Dearg Mor, over Loch na Seilga – summer

An Teallach from Beinn Dearg Mor, over Loch na Seilga – winter

not thought to be on ridges, yet how splendid in every way (and how popular) are the ridges of Kintail and Cluanie.

There is not much doubt that everyone knows about the 20, by repute if not from personal experience, but the 50 has some less-known names. Most of these I'd wager are Corbetts, or even lower hills like Morven of Caithness. Morven of Caithness is as startling a hill as Stac Pollaidh but does not have the misfortune to be parked in a lay-by. It remains relatively unknown. A connoisseur's hill. Sgurr Ghuibhsachan suffers from the same secretive quality and is almost a token gesture to an area, wild as Knoydart yet seldom visited except by the most dedicated of Corbetteers. The selection is in some ways representative. We have Ladhar Bheinn but no other Knoydart hills and, surely, Luinne Bheinn and Meall Buidhe out-class Ben Lomond or the Merrick? Yet with one Knoydart hill in the list, how could you leave out Ben Lomond or the Merrick?

Years ago when I made my request for choosing the best hills in Scotland two names came out tops, in a class of their own, and An Teallach and Liathach have repeated this victory again. They must be good! Ben Nevis has the advantage of being 'highest', not only in Scotland but in these European islands, but that is a mixed blessing. The special lure of the Ben has turned it into a cross between a fairground and the local refuse tip. The summit is a soured spot, like the oily surroundings of a garage, yet such is the power of the mountain (a combination of its dominance, prominence, and climbing history) that it rises above all else except those special two. The Buachaille I suspect comes in next, not just because of its scenic nature, but because of the associations the beholder has from climbing experiences. This was true for me: all my early rock-climbing was done on the BEM – and I fell off a route one winter in interesting fashion.

But something like that holds good for all the 20: people climb them over and over because they are such good hills then, because of the experiences as well, they return to them yet again. Humans have now become an agency in mountain erosion!

Lochnagar, Ben Alder, Braeriach and Creag Meagaidh are a bit like the Ben in being bulky plateaux with steep corries and cliffs, Suilven is reverting to the Liathach-type of hill, a speciality in the north-west where the tiered sandstone has created these pachydermatous monsters. Alligin and Beinn Eighe also fit this category.

Most of the rest in the Top Twenty are octopus hills: they have a dominant head rising from a spread of leggy ridges, or, to change the metaphor, they are hub summits, with radiating spokes. We think of enjoying ridges as well as summits when we head for Gillean, Bidean, the Saddle, Ceathreamhnan or Ladhar Bheinn. Cruachan, Blaven and the Aonach Eagach are ridges without hubs. The octopus hills are what they are, due to ice paring during the glacier ages, the glaciers biting further and further back till they had consumed all but an untidy core of rock. The same biting is seen in the big corries of the plateau-type hills. A few more ice ages and Braeriach would have looked like the Saddle. I suppose the ultimate fate of all our hills is to be reduced to a Geal Charn.

What a strange thing we have created. These 20 are 'mere protuberances' (Dr Johnson) – yet we have raised them to being something of a cross between gymnasium and cathedral. I sometimes wonder what the position will be in another 200 years, assuming we give ourselves that time? Will people still walk and climb for the good of their souls? Is it an assumption to presume there is *good* in mountains? They, surely, are neutral. A swallow doesn't list mountains and sheep would find lean pickings on our Top Twenty. These lists spring from the weird imagination of men whose attitudes to mountains has changed through the centuries and will no doubt continue to change. We no longer people them with dragons. Now the dragons are people.

Wheels within wheels. We sat marooned in a storm in the faraway Atlas mountains because of our experience of these 20, these 50, home products. Our diverse group's unity lay in a common serfdom of mastering and being mastered by these Scottish summits. When I read out the final lists one of the continentals, who had been observing our evening's extraordinary proceedings, blurted out, 'What language are you speaking?' I suppose what I've written here is the answer, by no means the whole answer, but the beginnings of an answer. The mountains will outlast all our games.

Camp by the Buachaille

So freely Glencoe gave those early joys:
the rasp of red rock
beneath finger tips,
the peppery sweetness
of blaeberry
on purpled lips,
the scarves of clouds
round mountain,
the wind-blown cotton grass
by Coupal Bridge,
the numbed pale hands
of a winter climb,
May evening air
like glass-bright wine . . .

The pleasures have not dulled with passing years:
the whispering wetnesses,
sighing moonlight,
wind's caresses,
young stars peering round
the Crowberry Tower,
the shiver of greenshanks' calling
through dawn's silk hour,
the fangs of Cruachan,
hazed hints of sea,
dewdrops, tormentil,
butterworts, tangy myrtle,
the flowers of frozen grass –
the little things of the long content
born of that brooding pass.

The Buachaille Etive Mor

Kintail in winter, looking to Beinn Sgritheall

MANY A MUNRO

These are pieces which describe specific days on specific Munros, or groups of Munros, all south of the Great Glen, that great division of our playground. They just happen to be places I've written about and their inclusion (or others' exclusion) is purely fortuitous. I always maintain there is no such thing as a dull Munro. Just dull visitors to them. Of course some Munros are 'better' than others but I've had dull days on great peaks and serendipitous times on hirsute heather dumplings. That's part of the fun, ain't it? The Great Outdoors Challenge (ex Ultimate Challenge) is a glorious way of Munro/Corbett-bagging without the everlasting car and I tell something of one of the wetter crossings from my tally before ending this section with a piece about some of the lessons to be learnt.

Christmas Peaks
OSLR 43

Because of the restraint of tradition it took a long time to break loose and head for the hills at Christmas, but for the last few years at least I have had Christmas Day out in the world of white wonder, a world of real peace, of wide-open spaces, quiet enough to fancy one could hear the stars singing. Not a telly or a mince pie in miles!

Our first Christmas away almost wasn't.

We had meant to be in the Torridons at a climbing hut, meeting in Fife on Friday 23 December to travel up on Christmas Eve. But early that morning the telephone rang and a Glasgow voice croaked an apology. His unexpected illness left us without transport but Joe duly arrived from Edinburgh and Derry from Methil. A big rethink. A bit of repacking. A rush in brother David's car to Perth just in time to miss the 8.40 p.m. bus to Blair Atholl.

No wonder people will suffer to own a car. The frustrations of not owning one increase as our services decrease. Public transport certainly was not much help to us marooned at Perth. However, a bus left for Birnam and once there we went up to the station and settled into our sleeping bags in the waiting-room. A brew on the primus after one o'clock and the train duly came. The pilgrimage to Blair Atholl was over.

It was breathlessly cold and clear. Our feet trailed a straggly pattern over the snowy fields to our camp by the river. We pitched the tent easily in the moonlight and lay back at last – with the murmur of the River Tilt beside us. An owl screeched across in the forest. The railway embankment lay behind us. You could almost feel the cold squeezing into the sleeping world. A goods train rattled by – loud and clanging in the silence. We were reminded of one of Thor Heyerdahl's experiences as a boy.

The future Kon-Tiki adventurer grew up among the Norwegian wastes, even then a tough and daring youth. On one occasion he had battled over some hills in a blizzard and come down into a valley where he pitched a 'bivvy' tent in the white, blinding swirl at dusk. The night was wild, piling the drifting snow deep over his shelter. In the early hours he suddenly heard the sound of a train. He tensed. He knew the line ran down this remote, empty valley but in the deep snow it had been impossible to locate. The sound grew. What if he had pitched on the line? Get out and run? That could be suicide. He lay as the noise rose to an overwhelming crescendo, the ground shook, snow spewed over the bivouac. Then the train passed and the whining emptiness swept back . . .

By the quiet Tilt we slept dreamlessly, waking later than intended. The frost was rimming the river with wafered ice which grew as we watched.

Cruachan

A tree creeper worked fussily on the pines beside the tent, so sure of its camouflage that I managed to photograph it from a few feet away.

That day we hiked 17 miles to climb Carn a' Chlamain – another of those elusive, solitary Munros.

Returning from Carn a' Chlamain it began to snow – pouring down for all the world as if someone had rent a pillow to smother us in feathers. Blair had taken on the look of Switzerland: walls, fences, every nook and cranny of every building capped with white muffs of snow, every tree had a white western side, every stone in the river stood out as a white hump from the treacly water.

Christmas Eve found the sound of the river completely muted while the moon swept long shadows over the silent valley. Every star throbbed as if the pulse of creation were being shown to men. It would have taken the psalmist – or heavenly choirs – to have sung that scene, that night, that joy.

The expectancy was still there when we woke, a long time before dawn. Beinn a' Ghlo was to be our Christmas peak.

It is a range, rather than one hill, for there are several summits to the wide-girthed group: a big, bulky area of mountains, steep-sloped, bitten into by 19 deer-hiding corries, rough with heather and boulders. In summer storms I have seen us crawling to the top cairn, unable to stand against a north wind (which whirled away a ptarmigan chick when mother exposed her brood for a moment). In winter I have met deadly cold that froze the drinks inside our rucksacks and sent us skeltering down before we suffered ourselves. The highest peak is 3,671 ft (Snowdon is 3,485 ft), and, if one of the more southerly Munros, it lies further from the sea than almost any other big Scottish hill. It merits respect.

It was still dark as we set off for our Christmas hills. We tramped up out of Glen Fender towards Loch Moraig.

By the time we had panted up the brae on to the moors (you can usually motor as far as Loch Moraig) it was full day, the first flush fading into the pallid winter light. Shaggy highland cattle were eating hay, the broken bales and churned-up snow making an ochre smudge on the white landscape.

The last of the trees were black against the cleft of Glen Tilt; ahead Carn Liath rose in graceful symmetry. We zigzagged up the south-west ridge, the only excitement being when an otter trollopped across in front of us, quite possibly the highest otter in Scotland that day.

In best Scottish tradition there is a false summit before the real one. On top a cold north-east wind had us pulling on cagoules, gloves and balaclavas. We ate Christmas cake, and admired the wide view – wide for, being a detached group, the sweep is uninterrupted. Distant Ben Alder could be seen as a white edge beyond whale-backed Schiehallion while Lawers, lacking anything to give the scale, looked for all the world like Kangchenjunga.

Scale can be peculiar. I always remember the story of an Alpine guide brought over to Scotland who, being shown Arthur's Seat, gave his opinion that the party would be hard pushed to complete its ascent in a single day – then stood on top of it half an hour later. How often we are caught the other way: judging Alpine peaks by our Scottish scale of things.

We raced down north to the sneck for the corniced ridge of Braigh Coire Chruinn-bhalgain. That mouthful translates as the *brae of the round, bag-shaped corrie*. No great ridge to climb, we still longed for crampons, for the wind had left the surface smooth and hard and we had to cut nicks with our axes all the way up; warm, rhythmic work. This second Munro is a great dome with biting corries roofed with cornices. Sun-warmed in our armoured clothing, we enjoyed walking around the rim. A sheltered nook called for lunch.

As we sat eating, we could look away up Glen Tilt to the gap of the Lairig Ghru, for the Tilt is one of the great quartet of passes radiating from Braemar on upper Deeside. Heavy snow clouds hung over the big Cairngorms like smoke over cities.

East and down (with false ridges to catch the unwary in mist) led us to the ascent of the easterly and highest summit of Beinn a' Ghlo: Carn nan Gabhar, *the cairn of the goat* – a very satisfying summit as our happy party stood on it that Christmas Day.

Our first two peaks now lay across a void, flanks plastered with wavy ice or buried deep in drift. To the other side stretched the soft landscape of the Lowlands. We lingered long before heading south to complete our circle. We passed over Airgoid Bheinn, a Top, appropriately the *silver mountain*. On its flank, after tip-toeing down the ridge a bit, we found a long shining gully which gave a perfect glissade down to the Allt Coire Lagain. A tramp round across the heather took us on to the rough road 'home'. Our feet dusted the white powder from the stems so a backward glance showed a brown track over the moor. Deer stood unafraid as we passed 30 yards away. The road ends at Shinagag, surely one of the most remote dwellings in the Central Highlands – yet a few miles from the vile, busy A9, which we reached an hour later. (Shinagag is now deserted, its occupancy ending with a strange murder case.)

The highway was churned up: black splatters of slush and dirt humped along the kerbside, cars flinging it up in dirty waves. A wild, smelly, world of noisy lorries and waving headlights. It jarred on our cleaned mountain senses.

We had Christmas dinner in the Atholl Arms. (Traditions are not so bad after all!) And in the tent, as the last hour of Christmas Day floated away down in the white-covered river, we lay content indeed.

Music

Music of the mountains:
Heart harmony;
Climbing in the roughest
Ecstasy.

A whisper of wind words:
Close cloud embrace;
Or wonder of waters:
Jazz-hot pace;
Or martial music mine:
Great crag cymbals;
Or morning murmuring:
Tree hymnals.

Dreams of a dreamer,
Drugged days of delight . . .
Music of the mountains –
Purging, light;
Secret and selected.

Personal choice,
Intuitive, inward,
Voiceless voice.

Music of the Mountains:
Violent vision,
Passionate, selfish – mine –
Jealous hymn.

Music of the mountains,
A long love awakening;
God knows the meaning, I,
spectating, I
Learning, listening,
Humbled low,
Must follow the music,
Must rise and go.

Loch Lyon

The Huge Concept of Beinn Dorain

OSLR 50

As you haul over the pass above Tyndrum for the long run down to Bridge of Orchy you suddenly see a hill of startling geometric symmetry filling the view ahead. This is Beinn Dorain, one of the most instantly recognisable of British summits. Hamish MacInnes describes it as a 'prodigious mountainous pile'.

This sounds a bit Johnsonian – but it is another eighteenth-century figure who is associated as closely with Beinn Dorain as Mallory is with Everest. Duncan Ban MacIntyre was born west of Loch Tulla and lived most of his life in this part of the world. Like many of the great Gaelic poets, his work is almost impossible to translate, and it is staggering when one holds a thick tome of his work in one's hands to realise he was illiterate. Late in life when he was in the Edinburgh city guard (and longing for his hills as only urban exiles can) he was seen 'reading' his poems to a fascinated audience – quite unaware that he was holding the book upside-down.

He 'wrote' scores of verses about Beinn Dorain for though he was an enthusiastic hunter of the red deer it was the wide, clean, free atmosphere of the slopes and corries that captivated him. Beinn Dorain has long been loved.

> O gladly in times of old I trod that
> glorious ground,
> And the white dawn melted in the sun,
> and the red deer cried around.

His was a freedom of the hill soon to be superseded by the rapacious sheep as men and beasts were cleared to make way for the Cheviots. He even wrote a poem in praise of foxes – because they hunted these interlopers! The sheep are still there, however, but not many people: Bridge of Orchy is a mere hamlet, where railway and road briefly kiss and part after squeezing over the pass and before swinging off to circumnavigate Rannoch Moor. The railway in places is actually floated on beds of birch, so impossible was it to find a bottom to the peat. You can feel the fall and rise of it as you pass in the train. The bridge at Bridge of Orchy was built as part of the eighteenth-century pacification of the Highlands. It is not a Wade road but the line chosen by General Caulfield, an overshadowed successor. When you lean over the parapet looking into the whisky-tinted spate, just imagine travel in earlier centuries.

It was at a camp in the wood at Bridge of Orchy in the 60s that I experienced my longest-ever shower of rain in Scotland. It poured for three days and nights, quite a test of schoolboys' camping abilities. Our old Black's Pal-O-Mine tents took it fine and eating, sleeping and chess whiled away the hours. At the end of the second day Angus Macdonald, the proprietor of the hotel (retired now) came over to suggest soup and telly in the hotel kitchen – and thereby began a long friendship. Camping here too we had a near-fire in a tent when a primus flared out of control. SOS procedure was immediately applied: a hand was slipped under the stove and it was thrown out of the tent – and straight into the tent pitched opposite!

When people ask me if I do not become tired of climbing the same hills over and over again I usually quote things like this to them. Every hill is crowded with associations, personal or historical. How could one tire of it? Routes change, seasons vary, companions are different. Hills cannot ever be the same. Beinn Dorain is typical. My first ascent of it was made alone, before breakfast time, having hitched from Glen Coe. The second ascent was made after leaving the station at 8.30 p.m. and we sat that night on the summit to watch a sunset of blazing splendour. I like it best in winter, when those pleated slopes are silky as wedding gowns and the summit rocks shine in diamond necklaces of frost. I like it in summer when the long days and half-nights allow all the Munros of the group to be traversed in a grand parade. The Bridge of Orchy Hills are like a knuckled fist punching west from the ancient Forest of Mamlorn. If once it was the preserved hunting ground of kings, it is now the priceless heritage of hillgoers.

Beinn Dorain is the eye-catcher and therefore the most often climbed. You can nip up and down between trains even – though it deserves better than that. The station is the starting point. On one occasion we arrived late and in desperation had to lay sleeping bags on the floor of the gents – the only place offering shelter from storms. (I noticed both of my companions went *outside* for a last pee!) Like thousands before us, we set off the next day up the Allt Coire an Dothaidh for the col north of Dorain. This becomes corrie inside corrie with the crags of Beinn an Dothaidh looming on the left and the lie of the land leading up to a real *bealach* (balloch) or pass. A couple of miles down the other side was where Duncan Ban lived for some years.

From this pass too you look over to Beinn Mhanach. If these hills are aptly described as a clenched fist, with four peaks facing out like knuckles to the Moor, Mhanach is the enclosed thumb. It is certainly one of those notoriously awkward Munros. More of it later. From the col the cone of Beinn Dorain has gone. I have shown photos of this rather characterless and featureless slope on many quiz programmes and never has anyone guessed the hill, so preconditioned are we with the conical shape. A wide, rather long ridge leads to the summit: a good viewpoint, as might be expected. Only the hills opposite can better it for they add Dorain to the view – but being below the magic old 3,000-ft mark, they are seldom climbed. From the summit of Beinn Dorain I once counted over 80 Munros and Corbetts and that was on a cloudy day when much of the horizon was lost. It is a summit for a good day and far horizons. The big hills of

Crianlarich, the Lui group, Cruachan, Blackmount, Ben Nevis, Mamores, Ben Alder, far Cairngorms; it really is a grand display.

Dorain's lesser brother, Beinn an Dothaidh (Ben an Doe-y) can easily be combined in an easy walk by returning to the col and going up it as well. On a misty day careful navigation is needed to ensure you reach the right summit. There are two bumps, and whichever you are on, the other always seems to be higher. Dothaidh is also bitten by cliffs to the north, Achallader, side: a corrie of tempting winter climbs that is seldom visited as the lie of the land just keeps it invisible from the A82. In winter both Dorain and Dothaidh offer unique bum-sliding opportunities for the seamed stream-bed runnels become cresta runs down which you can glissade with fearsome élan. This is an activity best left to the expert, however. I recall a friend once enumerating the types of glissade as being 'standing, sitting, fatal'.

Beinn Achaladair and Beinn a' Chreachain are often done in combination as well, approaching from the Achallader side. Requests to park at Achallader are usually granted. The farm is unusual in having an old castle in its yard, an historic one as it was from there the Campbells of Glenorchy rose to power, to eventually, under the title of Breadalbane (Bred-al-bin), own all the land from Etive to the east end of the Tay. It took many hundreds of years of course – and then all fizzled out this century. A long, canny ascent is advisable for Achallader's eponymous hill. In winter especially there have been several accidents on the steep slopes facing the Moor.

It was one such accident that drew attention to the shortcomings of rescue services in the old days and so helped in things being organised a bit better. Companions of a casualty on Achaladair actually sent a telegram to the Scottish Mountaineering Club's rooms in Edinburgh to ask for help. This was found lying on the mat some days later when the librarian happened to pop in for some books.

A pleasant route up follows the Allt Coire Achaladair to the col between Dothaidh and Achaladair from which, after a stiff initial pull, a pleasing ridge leads, in a mile, along to the summit. The view over Loch Tulla to the Blackmount Forest is a morning view while, northwards, the whole skyline is an etched array of hills with the Ben lording it over all. 'Forest' on our hill groups has nothing to to with trees; but it is an abbreviation of 'deer forest' and, as in the Forest of Mamlorn (of which this is the western extremity), it can be a very ancient usage. Many only go back to Victorian days when the sporting estates were created.

A marked corrie rim leads steeply down in a couple of steps to the Achaladair-Chreachain col and the corrie rim is cliff – which continues for much of the edge on over the Meall Buidhe spur and Coire an Lochain of Beinn a' Chreachain. This is the highest of this group of hills and has a de Gaulle-like, aloof feeling to it. About the only man-made intrusion is likely to be a train caterpillaring round the edge of the Moor below. The trees of Crannach Wood are a remnant of the great tree forest that once covered much of the Highlands. The Tolkien-creation of skeleton trees in the peat bogs is the main sign of this past glory for only odd reaches survive, or we see remnants in gullies where sheep and fire cannot ravage. All these cliffs offer some sport in winter without there being any super routes. It is too rubbishy to have summer climbing interest.

Sometimes Beinn Mhanach (Vannach) is added to these two, sometimes it is done on its own up the Auch Glen, sometimes as part of the grand slam. Rarely, if ever, is it approached from the east for that side is moated with the artificial arms of Loch Lyon and Loch Lyon is at the head of the longest glen in Scotland – not very helpful for walkers.

Park on the A82 rather than at Auch itself (the road is private to vehicles) and simply follow the glen to its triple head. There is a Land Rover track all the way now. Ais-an t-Sithein has no fairy ash trees of its name but is a smelly sheepfold – an ironic use for Duncan Ban's home, as he detested sheep and loved deer. Turn up the Allt a' Chuirn and climb Mhanach from that side – this adds the loch and big Beinn Heasgairnich to the view. This provides photographic stops, always an acceptable reason for a rest. If a non-active member of the party can be bribed as a chauffeur a traverse can be made through one of the cols down to Achallader rather than simply walking back down the Auch glen afterwards.

A tame driver would also be useful if setting out to do all the five Munros in one fell swoop. After various trials and errors my recommendation for this is as follows. Set off from the station at Bridge of Orchy and make a rising traverse to Beinn Dorain direct (a good test of morning legs!), then take the swoop down and up to Beinn an Dothaidh, down and up Beinn Achaladair, down and up Beinn a' Chreachain – by which time you probably will be creaking. Most cols have water on them, or by flanking along a bit, so there is no excuse for not stopping for coffee-time and lunch-time brews. Retreat back off Chreachain but then flank off Meall Buidhe to reach the col to Beinn Mhanach which is collected like an errant child. The going tends to be rather wet, especially if the white nappies of winter are still lying about.

The inward journey can be made down the Auch Glen to a waiting car or similarly through the Achaladair-Dothaidh col to Achallader Farm or, if carless, by flanking mightily along Coire a' Ghabhalach, an ankle-twisting exercise for the end of a long day. You would be almost as well going over Dothaidh again. Either way, Bridge of Orchy will be welcome. The bar well understands the needs of weary, drouthy hillgoers! They even have their own malt. Poetic stuff for such a hill of romance.

Ravens, golden plovers, deer and various wild flowers will have been a fairly tame haul of wildlife. Grassy sheep hills do not usually yield great treasures. The common animal of these hills is the frog. I do not know why some hills have plenty of frogs and on others you never see them. The same puzzle applies to adders. Some areas have them; some do not. Beinn Dorain has frogs. And if the deer set Duncan Ban singing of the hill, then Norman MacCaig, the sharpest of our contemporary poets with hill interests, has written about these creatures – another of those little memories we bear back from the heights:

Looking over Loch Tulla to Beinn an Dothaidh and Beinn Dorain

But clearest of all I remember
the Joseph-coated frogs
amiably ambling or
jumping into the air – like
coloured ideas
tinily considering
the huge concept of Ben Dorain.

Ben Alder from Culra

Under Ben Alder

I saw the stag fall,
Heard the shot
Tremble round these corries
Dusty with snow.
A grouse continued to gabble
And a trout held its position
In the peaty shadow pool,
A grey cloud chased a white cloud
In trivial pursuit,
A raven dipped a wing . . .
That was all the notice
The world took of a death
Under Ben Alder.
Would mine be more noticed?
I just hope to God
It will be as clean.

A Hundred Years Ago

OSLR 36, 43

Those of us who go to the hills regularly over the New Year are usually fairly philosophical about what may be granted us in the way of success, as the weather then usually stotters about between the erratic and the diabolical. Yet we still go (and are hammered as like as not) for it is all part of the game, as it always has been.

A century ago, a quartet from the Cairngorm Club recorded a typical Hogmanay escapade which is worth retelling. Their original ploy was to walk from Nethy Bridge to Braemar via Cairngorm and Ben Macdhui, a distance very few would care to tackle these days in pleasant summer conditions, never mind in the meteorological gambling season. In those days, no tarred road ran in to Loch Morlich, the Glenmore Lodge referred to is the present youth hostel building and between there and Derry Lodge there was just nothing of human construction.

They were bold lads, McConnochie, Rose, Tough and Brown. McConnochie was a great Cairngorms guru and some of his books on the area are still in print. (Anyone willing to part with his *Ben Muich Dhuie and its Neighbours*, the only title I don't have?) The names Tough and Brown are forever linked by their notable climb on Lochnagar, but they climbed in Skye and many other places too. Though they considered themselves chiels of the north-east, their account, by Willie Brown, appeared in the second volume of the *Scottish Mountaineering Club Journal*.

The party left Aberdeen on the afternoon of 31 December and reached Nethy Bridge at 8.40 p.m., the journey being made by train – which would not be possible today. Even by car it is a fairly devious, tedious run. They decanted into a night of exceptional darkness, aggravating drizzle and wind, the road sopping and slushy, and made for the Abernethy Hotel where they were well-spoiled by Mr Grant and went to bed with the promise of a 4.45 a.m. call.

Not surprisingly, this failed to materialise on 1 January and it was the late hour of 7 a.m. before they were off. The early start had been planned to fit in a useful 11 miles of walking before breakfast at Glenmore Lodge. As it was, that meal was taken at 11.45 a.m. as the going had been fairly demanding even then. They were walking on snow from the start, took a wrong turning at Forrest Lodge and above Rynettin, huge, soft, snow drifts were encountered, often forcing deviations from the track across the snow-covered heathery slopes. There was no view but, luckily, no wind. From

The vast scale of winter as skiers link Munros above the Lairig an Laoigh

Rebhoan (Ryvoan) through the Thieves' Pass, conditions improved and nearing noon they saw the reeking lum of Glenmore Lodge. Over 'breakfast' they decided the original ploy was hardly practical and, thanks to the local keeper offering accommodation in his house ('in view of the peculiar circumstances of the case'), they postponed the continuation till the morrow and went for a stroll to near Loch an Eilean instead.

That evening they were curious to see how their host and his family would celebrate the New Year. Brown reported: 'The entertainment opened with a dance, and concluded with a Gaelic song, which was chiefly remarkable for its extraordinary length, and its melancholy air. The singer, however, appeared to think that it erred on the side of brevity, for he apologised for not being able to remember more.'

The new day brought back the wind and the hills were blotted out in cloud. Brown noted they 'all displayed a marked disinclination to part company with bed' and they only set off at 8.45 a.m., having an hour of floundering through the snowy forest (no ski road then!), for part of the way using the furrowed track left by a herd of deer. Deep drifts made uphill work hard till the ridge path was gained. There the ground was wind-blasted hard and clear to give 'capital conditions' for walking. They dutifully noted 'Aneroid, 2,000 ft; thermometer 37 degrees'. No respectable Victorian party would have omitted this ritual if they could help it and a barometer is still a useful gadget and navigational aid, which I think we'd use more if it wasn't for the prohibitive cost. They were soon to be glad of their aneroid.

At 3,000 ft the wind blew the thermometer from their grasp and it smashed on the ground. By then the cloud was down too and they 'suffered considerable pain and annoyance from the small fragments of ice which the wind tore from the ground and drove in a continuous stream across the hill'. The summit was difficult to find in the near white-out, though the aneroid indicated its near presence. When a ferocious gust briefly tore the clouds apart they saw it just 30 yards away. They had thrown themselves face down on the snow to avoid being bowled away by the gust. They decided, with delightful understatement, 'by unanimous consent only to make a short stay at the summit'. One of them still persisted in noting the barometric reading while the gale raged 'with an excess of fury words are powerless to describe'. There was also unanimous consent as to the impracticability of continuing to Macdhui. Let me give a quoted, but condensed, version of the next bit just to show how little some things change in a century.

Readers familiar with Cairngorm will remember crags overhang Loch Avon with Coire Raibert the only opening through which a descent to the loch can be made safely had the weather been clear and the wind less violent, but in consequence of the dense mist and the drifting snow, which limited our vision to half-a-dozen yards, it was deemed more expedient to make for the head of Strath Nethy.

Accordingly, led by McConnochie, whose encyclopaedic knowledge of these hills is equal to any emergency, we began to move slowly in that direction, feeling our way with the greatest care, for this portion of the hill is bounded on the one side by the crags which guard the source of the Nethy, and on the other by an immense mass of rock known as the Eagle's Cliff. When 750 ft or thereby had been descended in this cautious manner, with numerous pauses to make sure that we were not approaching the edge of some precipice, a sudden rift in the mist revealed the jagged summit of Ben Mheadhoin, struggling faintly through a mass of sunlit and storm-tossed vapour, while all around the gloom was still impenetrable and profound. The effect was simply indescribable, and impressed itself upon us none the less forcibly because it communicated the welcome tidings that we were approaching a position of safety.

All cause for anxiety was now removed, for the descent from this point to the Saddle (the ridge dividing Strath Nethy from the Avon), and thence to Loch Avon itself, though abrupt, is perfectly simple, except when the ground is ice-bound. We found snow lying to the depth of several feet, and a good deal of scrambling and floundering took place before we reached the bottom. We arrived at the loch precisely at one o'clock.

Loch Avon was frozen over but not safe to walk on so they had to flounder along the shoreline, at little more than a mile an hour, to reach the Shelter Stone – in Brown's words 'exhibiting the gymnastics of pedestrianism . . . scrambling over rocks, plunging into and out of snow-drifts, balancing on slippery stones, and executing involuntary glissades – these were some of the feats which our tired muscles were called upon to perform'. Ptarmigan, unafraid, greeted their arrival at this howff and they climbed in for a cheerless lunch out of the incessant wind.

At 2.45 p.m. they were on the move again, a slow and difficult toil up on to the wind-blasted plateau of Loch Etchachan. The loch was frozen but left untested as the wind bullied them on, 'at a most exhilarating pace', for Coire Etchachan and the final descent.

As we entered Glen Derry it soon became apparent that only a small portion of that dreary glen would be traversed in daylight. Suffice to say, after much drudgery and many stumbles, we reached Derry Lodge at 6.15 p.m. and after enjoying an hour's rest and a warm cup of tea set out again, greatly refreshed, to knock off the ten miles which still lay between us and Braemar. These were accomplished without adventure, and at 9.45 p.m. (exactly 13 hours from the start) we were shaking hands at Deebank over a very mad adventure. Next day we walked to Ballater (16 miles), and returned by train to Aberdeen.

One thing that struck me about this expedition, as originally planned, was its sheer scale – with an almost casual 11-mile walk to breakfast and an equally dismissed 10-mile walk out at the end. That was 22 miles on top of traversing two 4,000-ft summits from Glenmore to Derry. Even in the modified form, it still indicates a walking power and stamina we could hardly match today.

This is no isolated example. To reach the SMC's Easter Meet the same

Kitchy posing with Cairntoul beyond: the view from Bracriach

year Willie Naismith and Gilbert Thomson walked to Inveroran (Loch Tulla) from Dalwhinnie, via the summit of Ben Alder, a 41-mile tramp. They started at 3.30 a.m., off the Inverness night train, and arrived at 8 p.m., just in time for dinner.

They were bold lads all right, all of them, with five-foot ice axes, tweeds and bendy boots, no crampons (and a railway system making it all possible). Let's hope a century hence we are still enjoying 'very mad adventures'.

Squelching Across Scotland

(1986's Ultimate Challenge)

'The year of the big black slugs' was how one weary walker described one of the very wet coast-to-coast events. The event experienced a new 'first' that year: nobody fell out with heatstroke. Tony, my partner for several other events (all heatwave years), now knows something of the wetter aspects of Scotland.

I had spent the previous 10 weeks in Morocco, where we saw rain on only five days, so neither physically nor psychologically was I ready for 13 days out of 14 being wet or wild, or wet *and* wild. It might have been good for the soul but it was murder on the soles.

As the event was my brainchild I was never in a position to voice doubts or despair. Frequently we met other participants without any inhibitions and I was blamed for blisters and bruises, battered tents and failed waterproofs, near-drownings and lost Munros. 'We thought of making a model of you and sticking pins into it,' one group declared. Perhaps they did. A stab of shingles, irritating 'nappy rash' and ever-increasing boot torture made it my most painful crossing.

Mount Keen from Glen Tanar

45

Tony and I met up at the posh youth hostel at Kyleakin, giving us maximum value for our rail tickets, made out to 'Any station in Scotland', a designation which drew comments from several ticket collectors. Skye was at its dreichest but we were given a dry hour or three for our run to Glenelg with Willie the post.

The waterfall at Glenbeag gained from the wet but exploring the brochs, the best on mainland Scotland, was a hurried affair. Up the glen a notice warned dog-owners that poisoned baits were down. We had a snack by the ancient fort, like a half broch, perched above the gorge, before tramping on through the wet for an hour to our bothy under Torr Beag.

Day Two began after lunch. Till then it had poured and we feared for folk in Glen Kingie and such places where spates and floods can present dangerous hazards. (I've lost as many friends to the Highland rivers as to Highland mountains.)

Our original plan just to wander up on to the Saddle and bivouac on the Cluanie Ridge was soon washed away. Eventually, in the afternoon lull, we raced over Mam Ratagan by forest tracks to the haven of Ratagan youth hostel. The rain rained and we morosely looked at the wrinkled sea-waters of Loch Duich. After two days we were still stuck on the west coast.

A morning's walk took us up Glen Shiel to the Cluanie Inn. With a B-and-B booked next day in the Great Glen, Tony and I were committed to a potentially hard day – and we had it, full and running over. We tramped up the old road for Tomdoun and then slogged long slaistery miles to gain the summit of Druim nan Cnamh, the first of the 12 peaks we'd require to claim a 'high-level' crossing.

For shelter we crawled under the main A87 Garry-Cluanie road where it stalked on pillars over a burn and made tea and hot apple flakes before setting off on a second Corbett, Meall Dubh.

This back shift led us up through a fine mix of clawing heather and sucking sphagnum to land us on the stormy summits just in time to meet the whipping of a sleety blast. Careful navigation was soon abandoned when a boundary on the map proved to be an old fence line on the ground. We sped down, losing height as fast as possible to escape to saner climes, then followed a burn down to Loch Lundie, a tree-edged mirror hidden on a plateau above the trench of the Great Glen.

Many years ago this stream had been noted as bearing a succession of waterfall symbols. While not seeking 'wet and wildness' we had our reward: fall after fall roared down in top gear. At a somewhat wearier pace we squelched several miles of track down to Loch Oich, the Great Glen at last.

Not being sure of our arrival time, or if our B-and-B would provide supper, I'd hidden an evening meal in the woods beforehand. We had a damp dinner, the rain pinging on the plates while we cowered under our brollies.

A two-hour dry spell took us up pretty Glen Buck, gave a glimpse through a gap to the historic Corrieyairack and then lost us in a welter of bogs and braes that drain to Glen Roy and uppermost Spey. By dour compass work, and a touch of luck we found Carn Dearg which gave us a definite known position again after our blind navigation.

We had brewed by a trickle of a stream, edged with snow, and this water we were to follow down to a bothy at the head of Glen Roy. Earlier I had walked in and left a cache on the east bank – while the bothy was on the west bank. This could well set a problem.

The first mile had us hopping from bank to bank but it soon became obvious that lower down it would be utterly uncrossable. Below the bothy another river plunges off the slopes of Creag Mheagaidh in the Eas Ban. Its deep pool at the confluence might at least be possible, even if it meant a swim. We had to have food!

So at the last sane crossing point I gave Tony my cameras, sleeping bag, etc., and went on down the east bank for the cache while Tony kept on the west bank for the bothy. Side streams gave problems. The main river surged down in Guinness black, with a good creamy head. I was well worked-up for an epic when I suddenly came on a bridge (not shown on the map).

The relief left me weak but rejoicing. I collected our food parcel, plus two bottles of *Neirsteiner*, and straggled into the bothy at the tail end of a wash of walkers. Several were old friends. The wine soon went, the quote of the day being:

The water has drowned the Matterhorn as deep as a Mendip mine,
But I don't care where the water goes if it doesn't get into the wine.

Chesterton

We messed messily under rows of drip-dripping waterproofs and the puddles of boots and stockings. The next morning we twined and did not meet again until the end, for they headed east for the Spey while we tramped a day southwards to Nancy Smith's hostel at Fersit, taking in Beinn Teallach (the new Munro) and Beinn a' Chaorainn (of the movable summit). We had a cold climb to the col at the head of the Burn of Agie and on the peaks it snowed on us – much pleasanter than rain!

An early start took Tony and me through six or seven miles of forest to Loch Laggan and thence up into the hills. We stopped at a sandy spit by a loch for the first really warm, dry picnic of the trip and, as a contrast to the snow falling in yesterday's summits, the cloud put itself through a shredder to open up a secret world of mountains.

It cleared on Geal Charn and on the pap of Creag Pitridh we could see all the whaleback giants of Mheagaidh, Ben Alder, the A9 hills, and the far Cairngorms. The clearance lasted all of 10 minutes. We traversed round and down to the bothy on the Pattack in the driving rain again. My brolly blew inside out and snapped its handle.

The one good day of the crossing took us over the Fara to Dalwhinnie. In blue brightness we actually brewed at the summit – and dodged the ice which was being blown off the massive cairn. New plantings now moat the Fara and, typically, there is no way indicated for gaining the hill.

Mrs Macdonald had a house full of Challengers that night. Several could be classed as 'walking wounded' but all were doggedly going on. Our route took us up Carn na Caim above Dalwhinnie but a tearing easterly gave us a tussle before we escaped down to the depths of the Gaick Pass and on, 'over and over', to reach a bothy just ahead of the trip's most violent storm. That made 10 summits done. So appalling was the weather that we abandoned our high route and walked out to the A9 and followed its route in to Bruar for coffee and Blair Atholl for lunch.

At one stage we had three roe deer dancing down the road in front of us. Despite being tired, we bullied ourselves up Ben Vuirich before dropping down to our overnight bothy. Surely we could manage just one more summit? We had food dumps on the Cairnwell and by Loch Muick for our planned exit via Tarfside and Clatterin Brig, but took easier options again.

While the next day did not lead to the end, it hauled that possibility into sight two days earlier than planned. We crossed a ridge after meeting three old Challenger friends and wended down for an hour of ease together in the Spittal of Glen Shee Hotel before shooting off in various directions. Tony and I splashed up a pass and bagged Monameanach, No. 12, before romping down into Glen Isla. 'Downhill all the way now, Tony!' We celebrated with a brew.

The glen was extraordinarily green and lush compared to our dark uplands since Laggan. We saw the first of many lamb triplets, a vast herd of 200 deer, and the river bank rang to the calling of curlews and oyster-catchers. We had five miles of green tracks but then the same of tarred road before we found accommodation at Kirkside House. We ate mightily and bathed lengthily. A call to the Montrose 'Finish Control' said 33 had fallen out this year and few had kept to high routes. There had never been such constant wet.

By dint of keeping to riverbanks and verges we both reached Kirriemuir still able to walk. We reached Forfar at six so I phoned Jim Cosgrove at Letham. Jim was one of the regular older Challengers but was sitting out this year – wise man. He was away next day but his wife Janet would have coffee ready. There was an Indian restaurant round the corner from the phone box and, as for accommodation, Bill and Barbara Redford had just finished the Challenge and would surely put us up in Forfar where they lived.

We paused at Dunichen to see a fine Pictish symbol stone and a monument to the Battle of Nectansmere (AD 657) before going on to Letham. There we hung up our waterproofs and puddled into Janet's house. Puddling off again was not such fun.

The last day is always road-walking and, by choosing minor roads, I've built up a tradition of buying and reading the latest Dick Francis paperback on that day. It usually lasted just nicely, but this time I couldn't read: the book would have pulped in a couple of miles. It was my feet that had nearly pulped, trying new super-light boots.

At Arbroath, our finish of the crossing, we arrived just two minutes before a bus left for Montrose and the social celebrations of checking-in at the end of the event. We received some odd looks on the bus. It took us a while to realise why. We were both steaming.

Lessons from Experience

This article was written after the wet 1983 Challenge crossing and appeared in The Great Outdoors *the following January when people would be preparing for the next coast-to-coast event. There have been several dry years since and one soaker (already described) but I would not change one word of what follows: experience is the surest teacher and the key is to THINK.*

'It had to happen one year,' and 1983 proved to be the year when the Challenge had one day of sunshine rather than the usual one day of rain. In some ways I was glad. Presumption is dangerous.

It was tempting after triplicate dry crossings, to be lured into a false sense of security, to leave this and that behind because it was 'never used'. But there is a limit to what you can do without – when the emergency occurs.

Tony and I went up the Ben on one of our crossings (we were staying at the CIC Hut) and, although we scrambled up Ledge Route on dry, sunny rock, coming down into Coire Leis we were cutting steps in a sand-blasting of spindrift. In 10 minutes, soft snow into which we dug our heels without effort had frozen hard as concrete. Thank goodness we had ice axes, even if no crampons, and the wherewithal to cover hands and faces from the flying particles. We then took the ice axes on a three-day tramp through the heather to reach the A9. By then they were superfluous and were gladly left for recovery a fortnight later – along with Tony's haul of antlers.

This year's change in conditions, and the comments of coast-to-coasters at Montrose, prompts me to write a bit on various aspects of longer back-packing trips. It need not be a Great Outdoors (ex-Ultimate) Challenge, of course. Nor even Scotland – but both 'Challenge-type-of-trek' and Scotland's meteorological instability makes this good training for any expedition anywhere.

I am actually writing this at McCook's Bothy below Ben Alder and the bothy book has a few entries from this year's challengers. Across the lawn is a new bridge over the Alder Burn. A few years ago one was washed away but the map still showed it of course. Being a dangerous torrent at times such a change could give rise to a desperate situation. River-crossings are no joke, but how many walkers have done any reading or any practice in this art? The map is not infallible. There are cases where bridges have been gone for decades but the map still shows them, while, conversely there are bridges not shown at all. I know one Wade bridge which is not on the map – and it was built over 200 years ago! Every bridge shown should be treated with suspicion in the planning stages and alternatives worked out.

Where rivers are shown as wide on the map they may well prove both wide and deep, and impassable. Plan accordingly. This is too big a topic to go into fully but most rivers and burns will only prove impossible when in spate, which is usually after heavy rain. You then either wait for the level to subside (a quick rise often means a quick fall) or you go upstream until the burn is tame enough to cross easily. If in a party, a roped crossing may be feasible but you must know how to do this.

If a river is normally impassable, it is often bridged for the convenience of the estate. The Pattack is an example: a whisky-coloured rush of water through a gorge – with bridges. Less easy are big valley rivers, often slow-flowing but black and deep. Glen Kingie is an example: in spate, crossing is hopeless down its whole length.

There is only one rule in this game and that is THINK.

The difficult River Carnoch was bridged by well-intending enthusiasts but, I feel, this is a self-defeating objective. There will always be one more stream someone will fall into or cannot deal with. Logically, all streams would end up bridged. Then where is the wilderness? Not everyone can climb Everest – but we don't yell for fixed ropes or a railway up it. Why then do we want to reduce our British wilds to the lowest common denominator – a dangerous activity for, when you rely on bridges, what happens when a danger arises and there is no bridge? Or it's been washed away? If you go to the wilderness, surely you go on *its* terms and you learn, by experience, the techniques needed. This requires patience and humility – virtues not highly regarded in this smash-and-grab world.

'Preaching', I'm afraid, is apt to sound arrogant. I have lost too many friends in the hills and had too many near squeaks myself to have any conceit. In May 1983 there were quite a few problems with rivers. I'll not say who it was, coming from Glen Tilt, who fell into the Geldie. An old hand, he soon had his tent up and was into his sleeping bag and drinking hot brews. Going 'arse over Tilt' was one comment on his ducking.

If 1983 set problems by water, the year before gave surprises due to the snow conditions. The first week in May often does give a last blatter of snow, but 1982 (and 1993) rather overdid it. Quite a few routes over the summits had to be abandoned or modified. This is the beauty of a multi-day tramp. Alternatives can be found to most circumstances. It is back to the only rule again – THINK.

It was noticeable that the bad snow affected the older challengers less than others. This is a classic example of experience bearing fruit. It was really rubbed in when George Fyvie, aged 75, came in with a high-level route completed. He cheated, of course, by having young Jim Cosgrove (a mere 69) to help him. That 1983 should see only 36 out of 207 starters giving up is also partly due to age. The Challengers' average age is in the forties. By that age a lot of water has flowed under your boots. And into them.

The weight of rucksacks tends to go down with age, too. You simply cannot carry so much. Yet if anything surprises me year by year it is the huge packs people are prepared to carry. Going by myself in 1983, my rucksack never weighed more than 30 lbs, even when carrying several days' food rations. You fight every ounce of the way as far as I'm concerned, even if this means a compromise. I had light footwear, no gaiters, no gloves or mitts, no ice axe and minimal extra clothing, so from Glen Feshie I had to tramp low-level to Braemar instead of crossing the crest of the Cairngorms. It was not a difficult decision as it was snowing hard in Glen Feshie, and I had already collected my dozen summits. They were not always the ones I had planned. Only Beinn Resipol was clear and I was chased off the Mamores by storms. Plenty of contrasts – and compromises.

Again and again you read in books the advice 'Never follow streams', which is as inane as any categorical imperative to do with hills. Frequently, especially in peaty country, the easiest and best route *is* to follow streams, closely, on a verge of green in the brown horrorscape. So it proved on the ridge west of Ben Alder. I followed the stream right up into the corrie, then broke up to the col between Munros 1 and 2. The first, Beinn Eivhinn, was thus done without rucksack. Aonach Beag and Geal Charn followed, but before number 4 I again left the load and floated up Carn Dearg. By this time my footwear was saturated so I changed destinations, dropped north to An Lairig and went on to Pattack where a bothy in a wood ensured adequate fuel for drying out that night.

The Blackburn of Pattack wood had 17 dead deer in it – the sad result of the cruel, long wet winter and spring. In the morning I heard the clink of deer hooves outside while still lying in my sleeping bag. Earlier, I had run into a blackcock *lek*. At a place I won't name, I watched two peregrines 'seeing off' an eagle from their territory – all wildlife interests enjoyed as a result of early rising and early going. (Blackburn has since burned down.)

However you have to alter and modify plans due to circumstances, however you worry away at logistics and routes, early rising is one of the surest aids to success. It is one of the easiest of assets, costs nothing – and is usually ignored. This is the biggest drawback to the comforts of B-and-Bs or youth hostels during a long trek – though even there you can work on it. At Acharacle I paid the night before, the hotel left out a huge cold breakfast and I slipped away long before anyone was up. Ardgour Hotel provided breakfast at 7 a.m. so I could catch the first ferry. At Kildrummy, I was on a farm and early breakfast was actually more con- venient. At youth hostels you can do your job the night before, simplify breakfast and have another on the trail later. The miles before noon are the easy ones. If the weather turns foul, the work is largely done. If it improves, you are in a position to capitalise on it. Strange how loath people are to grab the easy option. My earliest start was on the first morning, for overnight I had just slept under the stars – the only stars of the crossing, alas. That was furthest west, at Ardnamurchan.

Weight can be saved in many ways. Once, at Montrose, I was seen playing with maps and, in the end, I had ten 1:50,000 sheets piled up – the maps I'd used on my crossing. These I had posted along the way. I never carried more than two at any stage. They are cut out of the covers so I can fold them efficiently – and returned there after the trip. (Even covers have weight!) Some food, a change of underwear, film, an odd paperback – there is a gain in picking up items like these *en route* to save weight. One exception: if I can arrange real, wholesome food I see no merit in eating chemical-impregnated rubbish because it's light. As I was abroad until three days before UC83, my parcels were actually prepared in January and posted by my brother while I was still in sunny Morocco. There was always packing paper and stamps in the parcels so unwanted items could be returned home. Attention to detail is vital.

Posting is best done to hotels, or any contact other than a post office; invariably, you end up rushing to reach it before it closes – only to find it was half-day anyway. A telephone call to a local post office can usually make such a contact. Shops can be few and far between. I walked from Acharacle to near Alford in Aberdeenshire before I met a shop actually open. (What an indulgent spree then!) Campers can plan their days to come down to civilisation – Dalwhinnie, for example – during shop hours and then head off into the hills again. This takes a bit of discipline but it is rewarded with marvellous solitude.

Campers have complete freedom of movement and by camping (with the odd rewarding B-and-B thrown in) the best can be won from the venture. Tents should be light but strong and trusty friends, capable of taking a real skelp of wind or standing, dry, on saturated ground. Unless the ground is really soft, place Karrimats *under* groundsheets so as to prevent the groundsheets puncturing. (Camping in a puddle is no fun!) Use shelter, too. 'Never camp under trees' we constantly read, yet, often, that is the best place to camp.

Choosing a route deserves plenty of thought. You can go on working at this right to the day you set off. You will almost certainly modify plans on the way as well. Slavery to a route plan has caused more accidents than not having one at all. Weather and the physical condition of the walker are just two items which cannot be predetermined. Flexibility is partner to determination on a multi-day trip.

It astounds me how little homework some people do. There are even those who 'lift' a route someone else has done and described. As work output equals work put in, both in the physical world and the aesthetic, I would expect there to be much poring over maps, much reading of books and gaining general lore. It is much easier to learn by other people's mistakes rather than your own.

'Eat well' is one key. I have twice stopped my scribbling to mention to new arrivals that the bothy has a sack of potatoes, a dozen huge onions, margarine and whole bottles and jars of sauces and spices – left by some past mob. On the strength of these, I have stayed out an extra day and delicious potatoes, seasoned, and with marg melted over them, have been a memorable snack. Meanwhile, the others are tucking into curried monosodium glutamate. 'Yuck', as my school gangs would have said. Eat well means eating real food – not messed-about substitutes. There is no energy substitute. You waste calories to save weight and carry fuel to resurrect dead packets. For most people, a coast-to-coast trip is a special effort, an investment of most of an annual holiday entitlement – so it is worth making

The author, Torridon, Hogmanay 1994

it gastronomically special. The enjoyment should be in the doing as well as in retrospect.

Our passage should be quiet, blending with the natural world we are so much divorced from normally. Think how you can 'blend', for instance, avoid belisha-bright clothing and tents. Leave no litter – not even orange peel which, though biodegradable, will be an ugly intrusion over weeks and weeks. When you camp and use boulders on the grass, throw them back in the burn when you leave. There are many sites I loved as a kid which now are pock-marked and sick from such ill-use. Much of this is a matter of sensitivity, of thinking actions through. Ben Alder has a spade and the ground in all directions is soft, yet on arrival I found the back open stable had been used as a toilet – by dozens of dirty people. This sign of our passing is one which annoys because it is so unnecessary.

A good many readers, in the last paragraph, will have said 'bright colours are for safety' – a rule of the 'never-follow-streams' variety. Think a bit. For all the members of a party to be immobilised at once is extremely rare, so why should a whole gang parade in intrusive array? Even if alone, if there is need, *then* take out a bright bivvy bag to catch the eye. Till then, can we please treat the gentle colours of the wilds with some corresponding gentleness? I remember canoeing across Loch Maree once and climbing

53

the hills to the north, gaining a view of perhaps the greatest wilderness in Britain. In the valley below was a bright orange tent. The experience was immediately demeaned. The owner was, no doubt, given all sorts of plausible reasons for buying that tent (not all the sharks are in the sea). Alas, we are brainwashed and diddled out of many hundreds of pounds before we buy experience. This is why my one message is always THINK. Challenge those categorical imperatives. Argue. Complain. The manufacturers eventually have to supply our demands, not vice-versa. If we all refused to buy brightly coloured tents, waterproofs or rucksacks, they'd soon stop producing them.

It is not so long ago that one or two of us caused a furore by attacking all the sacred beliefs about boots. We even advocated wellies – and now we have Bogtrotters and Brasher Boots. Whatever else, a walk across Scotland will certainly test out your equipment – which is why your gear should be known and comfortable. Experiment when you are not committing so much to the outcome.

I failed to do this myself this year. My old faithful boots from Berghaus (which had taken me from John O' Groats to Land's End, besides three Challenges and much else) had been ceremoniously interred, and I was lured into trying a new super-light boot. The result was very wet, often sore, and eventually, blistered feet. I now know that for long load-carrying, super-lightness has drawbacks!

This does not apply to rucksacks. The fuss and fussiness of rucksacks is a wonder. The language and salesmanship has all the pushiness of car salesmen. You no longer just buy a plain sack to carry things. It is super-designed for soft egos and priced in the luxury bracket – so they sell well and the manufacturers laugh all the way to the bank. Years ago I found a plain sack and when they stopped making it ('Nobody will buy it now, it's not fancy enough') I bought several.

They eventually wore out. I now use Berghaus rucksacks. They still manufacture about the least complicated rucksacks I could find. I simplified it (and reduced weight further) by removing half the strap attachments. When manufacturers produce a sack which is truly waterproof I'll really believe they have our interests at heart. My most reliable item of equipment is an old fertiliser bag which lines my rucksack and keeps the contents dry.

Seriously, this is a vital point. Even if you get soaked during the day, as long as there is dry warmth at its end, the journey can continue. Plastic bags are a boon. All my food goes into them, which saves the weight of containers. Alone, a two-pint dixie cooks everything I need and its lid acts as cup, and if cooking while drinking, a disc of aluminium acts as a lid. One spoon does for cutlery. I don't fry, ever; it is a messy cooking habit. I save tiny 'ends' of soap. I leave toothpaste behind. I don't carry a towel. It is amazing how the ounces and then the pounds can vanish.

Even my first-aid kit lives in a plastic bag, though a few items are in an old cough-sweet tin. One of the greatest-ever inventions is Elastoplast. It may not be used for ages – then you never have enough. Carry a good supply. I take an elastic bandage and one wound dressing besides. In the tin are some creams (in tiny quantities) for the ailments which will vary from person to person. Whitfields I find excellent for athlete's foot (the price of having a shower) and I have Baby Wipes for bum rash – the price of being a sweaty human.

Nothing is more unpleasant than waddling along with this complaint. I've largely prevented it now by carrying a small sweat rag which sits in the small of my back and thus stops the flow. It also keeps the rucksack off my back a bit so air percolates behind it. Damart thermawear lets sweat through to the outer layers and Gore-Tex, of course, lets it out altogether when conditions are right for its system to work. 'Gore-Tex is magic. Sunshine is better' someone wrote in the comments book one year.

The body needs to be looked after on a long trek. It is just like a car, requiring the proper fuel and servicing. Blisters should be dealt with at the first hint of their presence – or, like rust, they grow. One or two people in 1983 suffered badly-poisoned feet from blisters. Wash and pamper feet as a rally driver pampers his tyres. As I look out of the window here, I can see one girl sitting with her feet in the bothy burn, a look of bliss on her face. That's worth doing a couple of times during the day; while the tea is brewing, perhaps.

From having looked at various bothy books, I see a good many UC83 walkers were glad of their shelter, either for a brew or instead of yet another wet night camping. As a 'thank-you', I think all long-distance walkers should join the Mountain Bothies Association; and also the Scottish Rights of Way Society. Between them they have made a tremendous contribution to the tradition of our freedom to roam in the wonderful wilderness. Both have modest annual subscriptions, provide useful information – and rely on such income for their good works. To save and renovate a bothy seldom costs less than £1,000 for instance, while Glen Tilt, Jock's Road and scores of routes have been fought, right to the House of Lords, by the SROW Society – a costly business even for the winner.

Most is commonsense, that most rare of virtues. I write, not from any inborn superior wisdom but from a richer, longer apprenticeship of suffering. I've made every mistake possible but, having survived them, I see no reason why others should be equally daft. Reading is much less painful. Whatever we do, we never stop learning. And what a grand schoolroom a walk across Scotland can be.

Addresses
Mountain Bothies Association, Membership Secretary: 26 Rycroft Avenue, Deeping St James, Peterborough PE6 8NT
John Muir Trust: 334 Grove Street, Musselburgh EH21 7JX
Scottish Rights of Way Society, Secretary: Unit 2, John Cotton Business Centre, 10/2 Sunnyside, Edinburgh EH7 5RA.

Please send a largish, stamped, addressed envelope when asking for information.

Crossing the Moor

Memory tends to gild its crafty frame.
Was that first journey over the Moor
Really made midge-free and legs unmuddied?
So it seems though I have returned since
To slaister many a way from Rannoch
Over to Kingshouse,
Red of face, swatting the evil insects,
Pitying the deer dozing on the thumb-nail snow patches
And wishing the Buachaille would lean
Its profile forward, not tease
With more miles than muscles cared for.
However, the sail of Schiehallion dipped slowly
Astern – and the Moor was navigated.

Just yesterday we made a crossing
And the lying brain
Tripped the green circuit of memory.
The blank screen was better: being there
With life to print afresh in forward stride
West, on the Moor, from Rannochside.

Moth in a puddle

BRAEHEAD, THE STORY OF A SCHOOL

My recollections of the hill days and other expeditions I was involved in with Braehead School occupy something like 60 closely written notebooks (out of a total for my adult lifetime of 230). Each of these books is crowded with memories as soon as I begin to dip into them. The first dip brought up the forgotten memory of an attempt on Macdhui one winter.

In the end we gave up our attempt on Macdhui. The snow was becoming so deep we could hardly move and, on those steep slopes, the avalanche risk was beginning to mount. Time to retire. I leaned on my axe, gasping for breath, both from the effort at beating out our furrow of trail and from having the blasting wind shove the breath back down my throat. It was an incredible turmoil of wind and snow.

One of the lads with me sidled up and, putting his mouth to my ear, bellowed: 'Is it bad enough, Hamish, to have to dig in?' The tone was hopeful. I smiled, not that he'd see it below the ice-clustered mask on my bearded face, shook my head and pointed downwards. His pursed lips mouthed a four-lettered word.

Back in the Corrour Bothy, the snow, still blasting past horizontally, we supped the welcoming brew and went over the day's adventure. I was struck then by how trusting they were (very humbling) but also how rightly confident, their morale high despite being caught by such severe conditions at near 4,000 ft. (A week earlier one or two had 'squatted' overnight in old Glenmore Lodge snowholes!) It was only back home, days later, that we heard of a tragedy that was happening on the same mountain, at the same time.

On the other side of the mountain a man and two kids had succumbed. New to the Cairngorms, new to the ferocity of winter on the tops, they had neither the skills, nor morale probably, to survive. The importance of morale (based on knowledge and experience) is not something I've ever seen discussed as a factor in survival situations but I'm convinced it is a vital one. All too clearly I could imagine a boy, battered and baffled by that blizzard, unsupported by the adult present, just giving up in the end. The kids with me almost hoped it was an emergency situation so they could deal with it. I'm sure the biggest difference on the mountain that day was morale. Braehead morale.

Another dip. The girls finally reaching the top of the Ben, some of them after two previous defeats or postponements because of bad conditions. Supper in the hostel that night was euphoric. Wee Caroline (to gain height) climbed up on to a bench at the table and threw her arms round my neck. I didn't need to dip to recall that. I reckon it was one of the sweetest kisses I've ever been given. Half a century later one of the girls on that trip met me and, recognition assured, her first question was 'Dae you mind yon trip up Ben Nevis?' Braehead memories, so bittersweet in retrospect for the school only existed for about a dozen years. Also, it was a meteor and its glow fell into the consuming layer of the earth's atmosphere.

Braehead School once stood in Buckhaven, or Buckhynd, as the locals more correctly called it, and was created as an entity to cater for the post-war 'bulge'. (The bulge was the baby boom that followed troops returning to family life after their years of horrible absence, and this, year by year, caused all sorts of demands – like the extra school places being needed.) The Braehead building was the old high school building but it had been so old that a new super high school had been built and some of the original was used by the local technical college. Come the 'bulge' and the condemned building was suddenly given renewed life. We were to be grateful for its antique condition.

In the new high school sticking sellotape on a wall was a sin; in the old we could do what we liked – and liked what we did. For the annual Christmas concert the whole hall, and balcony, never mind the stage, was covered in murals painted by the kids. And hardened critics came from London for those concerts. With hindsight, it was a good time, of hope and confidence, the post-war austerity gone at last, life there to be grabbed, the Beatles banging out the sound of it. How disappointed our prophet head would be to see the emasculated education of today, the grey sterility of it all sagging down from guardians who do not care for people or for the future. Outdoor education is a farce. But I rage, rage against it because, now, it is my pupils' children who are the feckless, flat-arsed button-pushers denied the most vital part of all – challenges to the imagination. Which is what Braehead gave.

The headmaster, the late R. F. Mackenzie, has written about his ideas and the school so I'll not do so here, other than to say that taking parties into the wilds of the Highlands and Islands was very much part of the school's heart; at any time a third of the pupils had been away on trips. I had whole strings of brothers and sisters coming up 'rarin tae go'. They were all people of equal value and what we did on the hills was just what anyone else did. It began as basically as one could imagine.

On our very first trip, to Glen Coe, staying at the youth hostel, I handed one lad two packets of soup and told him to put them in a pan. About five minutes later he was holding out the pan to me, the two unopened packets lying in it, with initiative enough to actually ask 'Whit dae ah dae noo?' That first trip was something of an experiment for I was given two real thugs (and two 'goodies' to balance them) with the remit to knock the hell out of them and see if it would do any good. It did a surprising amount of good and my report got them suspended sentences rather than being put away. Their quest for living had begun.

Donkey jackets and ex-W.D. gear, borrowed axes and crampons; these took them up Bidean gullies and along the Aonach Eagach. We climbed on the Buachaille and *walked* back to the hostel. No 'simulated adventure' for them. Years later I visited our county's outdoor centre and it was just like an extension of school, every day programmed out. If 'Canoe II' got wet, they could come in and have hot showers, then sit in the carpeted lounge watching TV till a bell rang and they trooped in to supper the staff had prepared. It was an exercise in soft living such as many didn't have at home but it had little to do with outdoor reality. Centres always struck me as being poor introductions, and, if proof were needed, in ten years our local climbing club received not one recruit from pupils inspired by going to the centre. Braehead had its own thriving club of pupils, former pupils, and invited friends – all able to do their own thing. School parties were often dropped off, say at Glen Coe, and then picked up again, a week later, at Dalwhinnie. In between we were on our own – expeditioning as genuinely as in the Andes or Atlas.

Somehow we begged and borrowed the gear we needed. Requisitioning 100 cricket bats was easy; obtaining four primus stoves took months of explaining, discussion, committees, even being interviewed – one such meeting terminated with one of the bureaucrats asking if we couldn't light bonfires and cook on them instead of having fancy stoves ... It was always a struggle but I reckon that, in itself, was valuable. People helped each other. Now, they sit back and expect it all to happen. With hindsight, the pupils who had the toughest introductions invariably became the keenest. In a recent discussion with some old FPs I was told, 'If you did it, so could we ... You never asked us to do anything you'd not do yourself.' Joe, on our very first trip, after swimming up several pitches of the Clachaig Gully (it was 22 January 1961), wrote in his log, 'To give Hamish his fun we swam up several pitches.'

I hated my own teachers as a boy because of their blatant insincerity (rules enforced on us could be ignored by them) so was very conscious of this with our gangs away in the wilds. They often amazed people with their confidence, and competence, even in things like cooking and behaving in a bothy. But why should a boy *not* be able to cook a good meal? The question is back to front.

We accepted weather hammerings then which would be regarded with horror by the educationists now. (Maybe the boffins' ignorance was our bliss.) Once, after a day on Narnain and the Cobbler we returned to camp soaked to the skin so, out of curiosity, we piled all our wet garments in a blanket and tied it up then weighed it back at school. Everything was then dried and weighed again. The difference, per person, was 10 lbs, which, in those pre-metric days, equalled a gallon of water. No Gore-Tex for us. But no identikit boredom either.

We once looked like being stuck in Knoydart by torrential rain. The bus was due two days later at Glenfinnan but the Carnoch River was in full flow. A trick of John Hinde's got us out. We had big orange bivvy bags so off came boots, clothes, rucksacks, and everything was put into the bags and these sealed. Once in the water they made fabulous floats and everyone just held on to these and paddled a long arc round the mouth of the Carnoch in the harmless waters of Loch Nevis. They were constantly made to think their way out of problems. I abhor 'rules', for the mountains keep coming up with situations not covered by 'rules' and then they find easy victims.

There was a classic case of some school kids who went astray in Snowdonia in cloud and pitched tents and waited several days for help. Thousands of man-hours were spent searching for them. The culprits even had a radio but, far from being interested in news or a forecast, they listened to pop till the batteries died. The news told of the search under way. When found they were actually praised for their behaviour. I asked our gang away at the time what they thought of this and got the retort 'The ejits should hae their erses kicked. You canna be lost in a place like yon.' But they had been, hamstrung by 'rules'. Had they used their gumption they could have been in touch in an hour. The stream they camped beside led down to a farm, a town, the sea. In Snowdonia you can't be more than an hour from human contact. But basics like that are lost sight of in the flurry of complicated navigation exercises needed to fill classroom programmes and timetables. Instructoritis can be a fatal infection.

This is no light matter. The watershed tragedy of the Edinburgh school party on the Cairngorm Plateau was a 'programmed' disaster. They were set to do a navigation exercise over the plateau that day and that was what they damn well did, despite everyone else finding their way off as quick as they could. To this day I'm often infuriating my parties by changing plans, sometimes again and again, yet, at the opposite pole, I've had broadsides condemning the rash things I've done with kids – such as the Cuillin Ridge. But this is the whole point. Nothing was ever rash (I'm too big a coward!) but nothing was/is ever so hard and fast that it cannot be altered to suit the needs of the moment. Braehead learnt this. Asked where he would have gone that so fateful day on Cairngorm, one of my kids grinned back 'The Aviemore swimming pool'. He was dead right. Sadly, others were right dead.

Those years gave me early grey hairs of course. I was almost glad when the school closed (the 'bulge' had passed and the mining industry had collapsed, at a local level with a tragic disaster at the Michael pit), yet, in some ways, I had very few really worrying times because the kids did behave, they did use their intelligence, they did THINK. I can recall, that first Braehead summer, how epic the traverse of the Aonach Eagach felt yet, a few years later, relative beginners romped it. We saw the whole history of mountaineering telescoped into a handful of years. In the last few years of the school's life gangs went off in the summer to climb in the Alps. The day the school officially closed for good we did just that.

We did a great deal of sleeping-out, bivouacking, howffing and bothying in the Braehead years. We had to with our minimal budget. But it was also fun. I wonder if future archaeologists will wonder at the odd circular walls dotting the Scarba shore of the Corrievrackan? Our kids built them to sleep in. Roofless they may have been but they were still preferable to the goat-enriched caves on the Jura side of the great strait. Snowholes were easier, they could be built anywhere. I recall one glorious climb on Beinn a' Bhuird's Coire nan Clach done from a cave which was half snow, half pink

Pancake night in the Blackwood Bothy, November 1967

granite. A candle in that secret burrow turned it into a glittering palace of white walls and rosy ceiling. Or the nights under the mouse-noisy Shelter Stone. I like the brief entry in the visitors' book that declared, 'It moved'.

Once we had tents, movement could be completely free but, with youngsters, systems had to be devised to minimise the loads carried. A tent on top of Braeriach entailed a considerable foot-poundage of effort. That particular camp was one of the coldest we ever experienced, as various details recalled would indicate: prunes left to soak in a dixie ended as dark objects enshrined in a cylinder of ice, lemonade under a pillow froze solid, eggs froze and even when fried, and apparently normal, remained crispy-centred. When someone spilt water and was about to sacrifice a vest to mop up the groundsheet he was restrained from doing so. 'Just wait a wee bit.' He did – and then simply prised up the ice and threw that out the entrance instead.

Black's Pal-O-Mine tents were our standard. We added angle poles for strength and extended flysheets round the back to ground level. If on a long trek, we'd take an extra flysheet and link this between two tents facing each other. With four kids in each side and myself in the middle along with the stoves we could largely contain an expedition under one roof. We cooked on good old paraffin primus stoves. They were safe. Even if misbehaving they could be controlled, usually. We only once burnt a tent – because the stove was outside. On a winter occasion when a stove was flaring the kid applied the ultimate 'immediate action' and put his hand under it and lobbed it out of the tent – and straight into the tent opposite!

The players were not amused. It landed on a vital school-championship chess game and they just could not set up the pieces again. Chess was a great tent pastime. At Bridge of Orchy we once sat out a 72-hour non-stop deluge and I think we must have played as many games of chess. Old Mr Macdonald, who then had the hotel, came over on the second evening expecting to find a scene of disaster. At the first tent he found everyone asleep, in the second he found several chess games in progress, in the third he was offered a cup of tea ('He looked so wet and miserable oot there!'), in the fourth he found me. 'I thought you'd be in distress,' he commented. 'But you're obviously all right. Bring them over for a bowl of soup later and they can watch TV if you like.' Because the kids were obviously capable and friendly we made many friends like that. Adolescent inhibitions mean little when there are shared enthusiasms. The crime today is that the inspiration is not given: false economy and moral bankruptcy.

At the end of a blazing heatwave trek from Killin to Skye we had a few days spare at our final camp near Glenelg. On one of these the local laundry van took us over Mam Ratagan which allowed us to climb the Saddle by a too-hot-to-handle Forcan Ridge. This mighty Munro is one of the few with a pool virtually on the summit. We didn't have much to take off before cramming into its coolness. Photos show strangely white torsos and brick-red or brown faces, arms and legs. We'd not dared trek without shirts on in case shoulders burnt and carrying rucksacks became impossible. In the Lairigmor from Kinlochleven to Fort William everyone, twice, jumped fully-clothed into pools only to dry off in minutes. Our Cuillin traverse was done in a heatwave and the commonest cause of failure on that venture is heat (if it's foul and wet you just don't start!) and this is also the commonest cause of failure on the annual TGO Challenge each May. When I did an account of our scorching day on the Saddle for a magazine I wrote something like 'We collapsed by the cairn and drank our bars of chocolate' only to see this editorially changed to 'ate our bars of chocolate'.

That same magazine also altered the everyday term 'bum-sliding' into 'bottom-sliding' – which took years to live down. That particular bum-slide was off Spidean Mialach above Loch Quoich and when we reached the lochside road we had gone through trousers, long johns, undies and some epidermis! I've photos to prove it. On a programme about birds one of the boys cheerfully explained that the name 'wheatear' was a ridiculous, meaningless Victorian euphemism for 'white arse'. The BBC, then very much in its Auntie image, cut that from the programme. It's as well they'd not got on to Munro names. Such as the equally euphemistic Devil's Point which, in the original Gaelic, is bluntly the Devil's Prick! Incidentally, behind the Devil's Point is Lochan na Stuirteag which is Gaelic for black-headed gull (*stuirteag* has always struck me as just the sound they make!) but the lochan is now the nesting haunt of the common gull. Did someone make an ornithological blunder, or did the common gulls take over from their noisy cousins?

But to return to our heatwave trek to Skye: after the Saddle we had another spare day before heading home so we wandered off along the coast on a shoreline exploration. We took our dixies so we could make a brew over a driftwood fire but by the time we were ready for this our dixies were full of assorted pool life we wanted to study further. One fish in particular fascinated me and, despite much shore work in the west, it was a complete mystery: it looked like a large tadpole with a polka dot on its back!

We'd paused in our walk as we were nearing the islands where Gavin Maxwell lived as we'd gathered he did not welcome stray visitors. But he was something of a marine biologist. He'd know, or could look up, the identity of our strange creature. I sent the two most diplomatic lads along with the dixie. 'And don't be long. We're wanting to brew.' A long time passed without the boys returning. Feeling a bit like Noah and his emissaries, I sent the two heftiest lads to see what had happened. They didn't come back either so we all trooped along to the white house by the ring of bright water. The door was open. I knocked and there was a yell to come in. We found our four plus Maxwell all bottoms-up on the floor which was covered with reference books. In the end the poor fish was dropped into a jar of spirits and sent off to the Natural History Museum and our tea was brewed more conventionally in Maxwell's kitchen. He enjoyed his visitors and asked us back. It became a habit; and many gangs were to stay in that beautiful place. And the poor pickled fish? It turned out to be a Cornish sucker fish, 'found only in SW waters and the Scilly Isles'.

That chance encounter led to so much else too. When I was looking for somewhere interesting to explore over a winter season I recalled reading bits of Maxwell's *Lords of the Atlas* manuscript at Sandaig and how he enthused about the Atlas landscape (as did Tom Weir who showed me slides of a climbing visit he'd made). So to Morocco we went, that winter, and the next – and over 30 visits since, often for three months at a time, till it is now my second home, the nearest exotic world there is to Britain yet, to me, as comfy a place to return to as slipping on an old gardening jacket: lovely people, spectacular scenery, sunny climate . . . We do, indeed, reap what we sow. The name of the seed does not matter. What comes up does not matter. But the tragedy today is that our education system is starved of resources. How can kids sow the future? We have used up the seed corn.

These seemingly random reminiscences demonstrate the lively, inquisitive, natural character of our kids. Some – many – of them were fanatical Munro-baggers but that was not the dominating be-all and end-all of their lives. They were receiving an education in the best sense of the word in that they were absorbing all manner of learning, 'without pain or pressure'. For a few summers we had joint ventures with Marlborough and Eton (the joke was that I went along as interpreter) and, each time, after the first day, the southern lads would stop asking me questions about their surroundings, history, wildlife and so on. They were simply turning to the nearest Braeheader for the answers – and getting them. Our boys and girls knew their country in quite a remarkable way. Years after our Cuillin traverse I was in a Skye bookshop when I had a tap on the shoulder. 'Hello, Hamish? Bet you don't remember me.' In fact I instantly recognised the lad who'd taken two others up to leave our vital water on the Ridge on the day of the heatwave. 'I'm married and have two kids now and every summer

63

we come to Skye for our holidays – all because of you.'

On another occasion a party of us were bound for St Kilda and (no uncommon event) had to put in to Lochmaddy because of adverse weather. It was Sunday morning. What on earth could I do with seven Americans there, then? I went up to the hotel to make a few enquiries and was immediately recognised by the owner, another former pupil. He had become a chef (in Buckingham Palace no less) and then moved on to become hotelier – and our saviour on a wild Hebridean Sabbath.

Food was fun with us too. There was no way I was going to eat at their standard so they had to learn to cook. And one outcome was that, with mining fading out and unemployment high, Braehead for years produced more people than any other school in the county who became chefs or such, an interest which began with making an omelette over a primus on Rannoch Moor perhaps or a curry supper in Corrour Bothy. Parental reaction could be interesting. I once had an irate mother burst into my English classroom complaining I was giving her laddies ideas above their station. 'Wantin Oslo breakfasts and omelettes an sic like things ah dinna ken. Gies me a red face.' She became more interested when she found we did it all on 6/- a day. 'A fush supper costs that!'

I only started keeping a careful logbook of hill doings when I began taking Braeheaders off to the Highlands and these books occupied a yard of shelf before the school closed. (I'm now on log 212.) The school produced a weekly newspaper and many a tale of Munros went into it. We kept school logbooks going too, and these battered volumes, a run of the newspapers and my copies of R. F. Mackenzie's books are now all in the National Library of Scotland. They wrote-up their doings because this was fun too. It wasn't 'English', it wasn't 'school' – but of course it was! And they learnt to read, to enjoy books, to use books. Reading night-time stories in the Blackwood bothy is an abiding memory. 'The Monkey's Paw', 'Ricky Tikki Tavi' or the *Chronicles of Narnia*. Most had such dull home lives then. And, I suspect, today's children have even duller lives, uncared-for at home and starved at school.

Our Killin-to-Skye trek was the culmination of a year-long project that began with the place-names of the song 'The Road to the Isles': the evocative 'Sure, by Tummel and by Rannoch and Lochaber I will go . . . By Ailort and by Morar to the sea . . .' – which led to the history of droving, to the depopulation because of the Clearances, of how history has left us the raw, demeaned wet desert of the Highlands. (At that time I took an English lady on a tour and she, a history teacher, had never heard of the Clearances.) One day a pupil was stopped on the street by a busybody from the education offices who demanded to know why he was out of school.

'I went to the library for these books for our project.'

The man glanced at the tomes the boy carried. 'What are they?' he demanded.

'Statistical Accounts for Inverness-shire and Perthshire. They'll gie me statistics on depopulation last century.'

That 14-year-old knew more of his own country's history and lore than did the questioner – as the latter admitted. The boy knew it on the ground

An ascent of Bidean by the NW Gully of Stob Coire nam Beith. Braehead pupils leading up Barclay Fraser

as well as from books. We walked the Road to the Isles, an experience that was to be a major influence on many of their lives, though we knew it not. The seeds were sown.

In those years we had few accidents (none of them real mountain accidents) and few social problems. The liberating effect of getting away was tremendous. Many had their first taste of the wilds at our Blackwood of Rannoch Bothy, a wooden shack which was largely furnished with bunk beds and other bits and pieces from the Inverkeithing ship-breaking yard. It had calor lighting and cooking and an old cast-iron range which did great service.

I've a picture in my eye of coming back off the hills above the Black Wood with a gang of happy Munro-baggers and finding one lad, who'd stayed behind, sitting by the fire alone. He'd made a vast pot of soup which sat on one side, the kettle simmered on the other, a pot of vegetables was ready to cook and a pile of wood chopped . . . Today there would be an inquest about leaving a lad alone like that. Yet that was all he needed, 'respite from pressure' in the head's words. He blossomed that week but on the last night he wet his bed and the cries of his nightmares kept us awake. We saw he went to Rannoch often; it was his lifeline and sanity, without it, goodness knows what he might have done. It always amazed me how tolerant and supportive the kids were with each other. This boy never had money. To get him away his peers would lay on a disco night and raise the money.

Accidents were few for, in the wilds, rather than at home, one automatically takes greater care. (For this reason going alone is perhaps safest of all – though the consequences of a mistake will be greater no doubt.) Most of our mishaps had a certain humour to them it seemed.

Hardly a mountain accident occurred at the Steall Hut – a rope swing broke and a lad crashed to the ground. I was over at the foot of the falls with some of the party so did not hear the yells from the hut but gesticulating figures did catch our attention. By the time we arrived Bill was sitting sipping tea with his arm in a sling. I wasn't really needed. Who came up with the solution of a blanket for getting him across the river I can't recall. It worked but, in November, was not much fun. Nor was carrying Bill on my back down the icy gorge. Luckily, for the first-ever time, we had our school bus with us for the whole period so he was soon in the Belford Hospital.

In those days there was a deeper pool at the wire bridge and by fixing up a long wire (a detached stay for the bridge) we could snap on a sling and karabiner and zoom down, letting go halfway, to land with a great splash in the pool. The lower end was anchored on the bank beside a wide spit of gravel and one lad, losing heart over the water, held on – a big mistake – for he was dragged up the gravel by the force of his momentum. Actually he was lucky; he was dragged along on his back and had plenty of skin removed from the nape of his neck to his heels. Even his swimming trunks were ripped off.

'Just think if he'd gone along on his tummy!'

None of the abrasions turned bad and his worst inconvenience was the crinkling of scabs whenever he moved. He had my sympathy on that. A lad once placed my soup behind me in the tent and, not knowing, I sat in it. So I know about crinkly scabs. Perhaps the nastiest scalding we ever had (the only one I can remember in fact) was when we were camping on Rum and someone tipped the porridge pot on to his thighs. Considering we always cooked on paraffin primus stove, we had very few mishaps. The Scout manual's advice to always cook outside used to give us a chuckle: obviously written for sunny southern, summer use. Try that on Rannoch Moor in a February blizzard.

At Steall, too, a teacher came to grief on that wire bridge. With poor eyesight, at night, she stepped into the gap at the far end where the foot rope spread out in a V and went drifting off downstream (dutifully bleating 'Help!' six times a minute). When she crawled out the worried dog promptly bit her.

The only tent which ever went on fire did so because, for a moment, nobody was in the tent. The lad's exit to fetch water had rubbed the doorway which unfurled without his noticing, a gust of wind blew the canvas out, then back inside – across the flame. It ignited at once and in seconds the whole tent was ablaze, a useful object lesson in the way no theory would be. In the Alps I had my only personal experience of a tent going up, thanks to someone dropping a gaz *cartouche* when changing over. As there were candles lit and another stove going, two of us and the culprit simply dived for the exit and had our progress speeded by the blast. After that nobody, ever, changes a gaz stove inside a tent or building; if they refuse to go out, then I will. For we met, rather than experienced, a horrendous accident near old Steall.

We were carrying loads up to the camp on a smooth 'lawn' near this ruin (I can recall using it as a bothy) when we saw a column of smoke rise into the air. Curses! It appeared someone already had the site. Still, a fire might help keep away the midge menace. We went on and, arriving, found another school party in a dreadful state. Someone was changing a gaz stove in a tent beside another lit stove, made an error, and there was an instant explosion. We had to deal with faces which had run down on to chests and melted clothes.

In this area we once made a school summer traverse of the Grey Corries. There were odd snow patches remaining and these were brick hard. One lad assumed that it was the usual soft snow he'd always experienced and took a flying leap on to the top of the slope – and went shooting off downwards. He soon turned head-first, sweets emptying from his rucksack pockets, and crashed on to the boulders below. The rest of us rushed round to reach the figure. The fleetest of foot went past the prone figure and started picking up the sweets. When taxed later he replied, 'Och sir, I knew *he* was all right. He landed on his heid!'

Very early on in Braehead's days we had a near thing which had the hairs on my neck stand on end. (Some wonder why 12 years of Braehead turned my head grey!) We were climbing Aonach Beag. The final dome was deep snow and the cloud was down so visibility was next to nothing, ground and sky all blazing white – a dreaded white-out. Trusting my navigation's

A Braehead lad climbing on Sheepflank Wall, Polldubh, Glen Nevis (early 1960s)

accuracy, we advanced slowly for I knew the cairn stood on the edge of the precipice and it wasn't a very big cairn. I was standing irresolute, about to turn back for safety, when Mike drifted past me a step or two. In that instant I saw, below the frozen surface, blobs of orange peel and a greying of stones. In a flash it came to me that people ate oranges at the summit. We were there. The depth of snow covered the cairn. I yelled at Mike to stop. He did and there, a couple of steps ahead, was a dim horizontal line, the edge of the cornice. He took two of the gentlest (and eternal) steps back to the safety of the blessed litter-spot. That and a canoeing near-accident are the two closest encounters with fatality we had in the Braehead years. It could be argued of course that no youngsters should ever be on the hills in winter. Given a few summer accidents, of course, the argument could shift. They shouldn't be out in summer. Today's safety at all costs has killed the mountains, not people. It is all much safer on television. Give them simulated adventure. As if you can fool kids like that.

Mike was an exceptionally able mountaineer (or he wouldn't have been with me at all) and decisions as to what we did took that into account. I just wish he had become an outdoor instructor for he had the patience and helpful approach which is natural, not taught. He did much with a friend Joe, the better climber, but bold and his own man. They made quite a team. Just after leaving school they joined me for a weekend bus outing to Glen Coe with a local mountaineering club – one long defunct. We planned the winter classic of the North Buttress on the Buachaille.

The Buachaille was plastered high up but blacker below. Very wintry at all levels. On the bus run up a solitary English lad approached us and asked if he could join us. He was new to Fife and alone. I quizzed him as to his climbing and he mentioned names of routes in Wales and the Lakes which I knew from reading. He had a rope and gear. He appeared to be OK. And two ropes of two would make much better time than a cumbersome trio. He and steady Mike could team up. I'd take Joe and give him some leading to do if possible. I assumed the other would lead his rope.

We moved, unroped, up the early stages, the rock being nowhere difficult. The newcomer seemed OK and he roped-up with Mike without delay. We roped when the route steepened and because the rocks held *verglas*, wicked ice that barely showed against the rock, so one had to be very careful not to step or pull on anything untested. Mike later commented how often the best way to ensure a hold was safe was to hold it long enough so the skin of ice would melt – then it was safe to stand on.

So we took our canny routes, parallel but often invisible to each other, but Joe and I soon drawing ahead. We then had to wait a cold and miserable hour before the other two appeared. Mike was leading. He came to a good spike and belayed, then yelled to his partner to climb when he was ready. After a long pause a none too cheery 'Climbing!' drifted up. He was unbelievably slow and Mike had to tell him where to put practically every hand and foot. He talked the man up. 'That wasn't so bad, eh? . . . there's a wee nick roon the corner. Wedge yir toe in it . . . Noo, that knob there, I bashed the ice off it . . . give a good pull . . . well done . . .'

Joe and I raised eyebrows at each other – and kept quiet. Mike was 16 at most but utterly at home. His partner, so sure in the bus, was later to confess he had never seen *verglas* before. It was the first, but not the last time, we had trouble when adults joined us under false assumptions that they had to be better, more mature, the boss, where in fact the youngsters were far safer and superior.

I wish I had written more about Braehead at the time or just after the school closed. Its humanity of course would be anathema to the uncaring, selfish society created in the last decade, a decade that sees far more vagrants sleeping rough in the streets of London than sleep rough in Marrakech. Pupils leaving Braehead to go to 'the other place' to continue their education hated it for its insincerity: on to higher education they found they were treated like kids, not people, not individuals. But then the major point of education is to turn out docile conformists. We are as manipulated a society as any other. I really feel sorry for children today.

We once coincided with the High School at Loch Morlich youth hostel where I regularly had ski groups. We began that activity by making our own skis, then we were lucky enough to buy the annual reject stock from Glenmore Lodge. (Replacing edges is a task I'd be happy to forgo during whatever life is left to me.) Our boys and girls were already hill-orientated so skiing to them was an extension of experience: Munro-bagging rather than piste-basking was their joy – as soon as they could control their flippers. Many a night they bivvied out in the lodge's snow holes in Ciste Mherard or stood by Macdhui's cairn hoping to encounter Ferlas Mor. Skiing – like canoeing – was a means to an end not an end in itself.

It was a matter of pride to be first on the slopes and last off them. We worked. At the end of each day we'd return to the hostel, one half of the group immediately starting on preparing supper, the other half showering, then swopping over. An hour after our return we'd sit down to an excellent meal. An hour after that most were drifting off to bed as eyes just would not stay open over chess boards or whatever . . . It was something of a puzzle why ski hostels had extra late hours.

This weekend we arrived back as usual to find the kitchen in uproar. There was another school party in and it proved to be the High School. If ever a night proved points it was to be that one. What annoyed me then, and still does in so many comparable situations, was the assumed superiority of one of the parties. Braehead was only a junior secondary so the High School naturally looked down on us. When we sat down to eat that night our normal, quiet, family atmosphere was shattered by yelling and shouting from the other gang of hooligans. The teacher with them did nothing to stop it.

We had dormitories next door to each other, and walking down the corridor that evening I was tailing two of their big louts when one of our mites came out from our room. The two, unaware that I was behind them, immediately set on my lad and starting kicking him in. The odds changed somewhat when I joined in! (Oddly enough a version of this incident was told to me by someone else just last year.) We were all abed by nine o'clock but were woken later on by the din from next door – which then went on for hours. In the end I stormed through and read the riot act. It was only on the way out that I realised the bed nearest the door was occupied by their teacher!

On a lighter note, we were once staying at Glen Nevis hostel with a girls' party and they had not appeared as planned in the morning. Told of the problem, Davy, the warden, told me just to go in and wake them. It was only after cheerfully bouncing three scantily-clad girls on to the floor that I realised none of them was mine! Our girls that day at last fulfilled an ambition and reached the summit of Ben Nevis. That was the time tiny Caroline climbed on to a bench to throw her arms round my neck. Our kids *lived* and such have no need to riot, to be obnoxious. We reap what we sow.

I don't claim our pupils were paragons. Once, when I had a class for English in my first year, there was such a racket coming from the class next door that I went through to shut them up. I found their teacher standing pale and helpless at his desk, facing a pack of wild dogs – who immediately subsided into order when I banged in. Very embarrassing.

My head of English had frequent cause to lecture me no doubt but his reputed admonitory introduction 'I've been teaching for 30 years so I should know' was not the best inspiration. On one occasion I was given dire warning that an inspector was coming next day. Whatever I was doing, when he came in with the inspector, we were to be on a certain page, doing a well-rehearsed exercise. 'You'll know it's the inspector because I'll give three sharp knocks on the door. And be on *your* best behaviour. Call the inspector "Sir" always . . .' (I forget the rest of the briefing.)

The knocks duly occurred, the door was flung open with stagy vigour. 'Mr Brown, the inspector.'

The inspector walked in, looked at me, did a double take, then grinned broadly, 'Oh hello, Hamish, I was hoping it might be you. How's life?' He shook my hand vigorously while my head looked on like a codfish, open-mouthed.

The inspector had, not long before, proposed me for the Scottish Mountaineering Club, of which he was a member. We had climbed many a Munro together. Dear Barclay Fraser. He was one of the kindliest people I've ever known. I'm amazed, now, that he should have ever countenanced the maverick young Broon and I owe him a great debt for his quiet example – the best teaching method there is really. We were to roam the hills of Corsica, the Pyrenees and High Atlas in the years ahead as well as sharing a love of all things Scottish. As an elderly man he tumbled down a flight of stairs and broke his neck but, after lying immobile for months, fought back and stood again on top of Munros. That was teaching too! In his mid-eighties a brain tumour developed. We spoke on the telephone before I went off to Morocco for several months. His speech was slurred but the words kind as ever: greetings to folk at Imlil please, recalling the incomparable view from Mohammed's house. It was at Mohammed's house that I had the news that Barclay had died. And this is written at the same spot, with tears. When I told Barclay about the careful set-up for his arrival in my classroom there came a twinkle in his eye. 'Why do you think I gave you such a hearty greeting, Hamish?'

A Braehead trio nearing the summit of the Buachaille Etive Mor, 1968

Gradually the head gathered an enthusiastic staff who were prepared to avoid the double standards, which was largely what Braehead was about. Let me illustrate with one perennial issue – smoking. In the school's last year or two I doubt if ten out of 700 smoked, an exceptional figure. How did it come about? By the usual punishments, suspensions, expulsions? No.

The staff felt strongly enough on the matter to screen an anti-smoking film which climaxed with a lung-cancer operation. (As the blood welled along behind the scalpel stroke two teachers passed out. The kids loved it.) The deputy head gave a talk one day at assembly and was given no great attention. He asked some seniors what had been wrong with what he'd said. The reply was 'There was nothing wrong wi what you said sur, but look at yir fingers.' They were stained with nicotine.

'You're quite right. Who am I to preach to you when I can't control myself? I'm sorry. I'll never mention it again.' Nor did he. Smoking is largely a gesture at that age, a kicking against the pricks. When there are no pricks, kicking is wasted effort. We believed hypocrisy a greater sin than smoking. Tackling the former dealt with the latter.

Our outdoor doings helped too, for it was astonishing, at the end of a long hill day, to find the party always returning in two sections (What I called 'the quick' and 'the dead') and the laggard section invariably was composed of the smokers. They read the lesson. Sermons weren't needed. I remember once, in my room (known as the Howff) when we were busy drying tents and such tasks one lunch interval, a boy pleaded, 'Oh Hamish, would you mind if I had a smoke. I'm gasping.'

Before I could reply half a dozen voices snapped, 'You're no smoking in here . . . Aye, we'd mind . . . Don't be effin stupid . . .'

Often enough I'd be in early and would like to have put on a brew only to find no matches anywhere. I could lean over the balcony of the hall and yell, 'Can someone please let me have a match?' and, with no feeling of guilt or fear someone would throw up a box. That was a far healthier relationship than the fear and hypocrisy surrounding smoking in schools normally. We had an amusing incident on these lines once at the Maiden Rock near St Andrews.

This sandstone pinnacle gave an excellent 'climbing wall' before such were invented and we often went there for the day. In the morning half the group would climb while the rest explored the coast and staggered back under huge loads of driftwood. In the afternoon the groups would change over then, at the end, we would have a mighty bonfire and toast sausages and boil billies of tinkers' tea – only on one occasion we found none of us, ten in all, had any matches. It happened that a Madras College class was filing along the high path above the Maiden Rock so I told one lad to nip up to them and get a match or two off someone. Our courier only went halfway before puffing to a stop. He yelled up, 'Ony of youse got a match?' The result was a comical confusion, a turning of heads, a hurrying on. I

A cheery Braehead gang on top of Schiehallion, 1969

called the lad back and pointed out that their teacher had also heard the request and anyone with matches would be in certain trouble. 'Go up and ask quietly.' He did and returned with a few matches. 'Whit sort of daft set-up's yon?' he asked me. Alas, it is the way the world works. School is training for it after all.

On one of our earliest trips to Glen Coe we once got a lad up the Pap of Glencoe by assuring him there was a café on top and he'd be able to buy fags there. He was quite a nasty bully and at a loss how to take the hilarity at his summit discomfiture. We always stayed in the hostel, then under the rule of Ingrid and Jim Feeney. Big Ingrid was 'auntie Ingrid' to many of our gangs. This same lad was giving her cheek one night from what he considered the safety of the stair up to the men's dormitory. Ingrid simply pursued him and returned, dangling the lad upside down at arm's length, gave him a good walloping on his backside and dropped him on the floor. (Ingrid was, in the words of another lad, 'six foot – in aw directions'.) But the same Ingrid was to hug him on leaving and he took every chance of returning to see 'the first decent person I've met'. He came to me one night and said in awed tones, 'They ken I'm here an they still leave the till drawer open.' Poor Darkie; that week turned his world upside-down. On the run home he tried to bully one wee lad only to be told to shove off. He did.

When anyone reached the 50-up of Munros we made something of an event of it. They received a special badge, a book of Tom Weir's signed by the author and the then Sir John Hunt (who'd written a preface to the book) and, my treat, a slap-up dinner somewhere special. (Latterly most of these were saved and taken in the Alps.) Once Ingrid visited the school and was taken on stage to present these honours. In her uninhibited way she didn't just shake hands with the first lad up, she smothered him in a hug. The boy went scarlet, then grinned and returned the gesture while 700 hooted with glee. On a separate occasion there was one boy, a tiny lad with buck teeth, timid and likely to be dismissed elsewhere, who had reached 47 Munros and the family were off to live in Australia. He'd miss his 50. So it was decided to give him rewards anyway. He left the stage in a daze, eyes streaming, while the school cheered him back to his seat. Often a class would run a dance (disco) to raise the cash to send one of their number on an expedition. It was a very special place.

The school bus being much used, parties were taken to some place in the Highlands and then picked up at another spot ten days, or whatever, later. In between, we were on our own, self-contained, self-propelled, whatever wind, rain, snow or midges might do. I persuaded as many other teachers as possible to come along too. It was the quickest way to silence the grins that my work was just one long holiday. The head, R. F. Mackenzie, needed no persuading. He'd try anything and everything – once anyway – so we scared the shit out of him on the Buachaille, near drowned him canoeing across Rannoch Moor and had him spewing in David Haye's boat bouncing over the Dorus Mor to Scarba. As far as I know, my appointment was the first in a Scottish state school to do what would develop into outdoor education. My remit to 'take the boys and girls of Braehead School into the wilds and do what I liked with them' had teachers suggesting specific nasty things to do to some of them. But that worked both ways too. I once lay in a tent listening to a conversation in the next tent (kids seem to think tents are soundproof) where they were making up 'ropes' of teachers they'd take up on the Ben – then cut the rope!

For some time we had a head of English named Laurie Campbell and he, several times, drove our parties up to Ingrid's (Darkie often just coming for the ride to see 'auntie', having a 'respite from pressure' day in the evocative term coined by R.F.). Laurie was a great yarner and would tell all sorts of tales of his past. That we had a different life story every run did register with me but seemed of little account. The name also rang a bell somewhere. I'd known a Laurie Campbell in the past. Life was too busy to make connections. Then, suddenly, we had a new head of English, replacing Campbell, who had been pretty good at that job but had been stealing typewriters and then proved to have several wives, which is not allowed. All came out in the end.

When I was doing National Service in Kenya there were several civilians who generously opened their homes to servicemen. One was a headmaster of a local school, one Laurie Campbell. Our head of English had been one such serviceman (I was another) and he had gone through his host's papers and copied all the details. Years later, he applied for this teaching post at Braehead, claiming he had just escaped from the horrors of the Congo where he'd lost all his documents, but they could check the facts he gave – Laurie Campbell's in fact – which checked, were all right of course. He got the job!

Over the years many articles of mine about Munros and the wilds of Scotland described school expeditions without their ever being specified as such. That they were kids doing what was described was immaterial to me but might not have been so to editors or readers. Braehead doings in the wilds were no different from anyone else's which was precisely why we did them. Far from being pests, intrusive, noisy, etc., they often were superior to many adult parties. They were more responsible, not less, far more cheery and uncomplaining. And, socially, far less obnoxious (no drunken bothy nights!). So, to finish off this section, here are two very different articles which were specifically about them, as school parties.

75

Braehead skiing on the Cairngorms – looking to Maedhui

Snowed-in at Glendoll

The 12 years when I took youngsters into the wild high places of Scotland occurred long before outdoor education became the ogre many see it as today. Operating within the tight social loyalties of one school, the atmosphere was one of voluntary enthusiasm. It was great fun. Many of the girls and boys from 30 years ago are still climbing friends today, in contrast to the dismal lack of enthusiasm and continuity one sees in the mass approach nowadays. You cannot, basically, *make* outdoor types. It will out if it is there, for most of us seem to manage to get the things we most want. The sadness of life is that so many want so little.

In all those years we only twice failed to return to school on time at the end of a trip. (None of those high-falutin' 'expeditions' or 'curricular experiments in physical skills'.) The first was due to being marooned on Jura by storms when the boat couldn't risk the Corrievreckan, the second was when we were snowed-in in Glendoll. Unlike most citizens, hillgoers like good bad winters and this gang was staying in the Carn Dearg club hut in Glendoll and had taken skis hoping for good snow.

The snow was well down already and the frost was keen. Great to squeak up the road to the farm for eggs, Creag Mellon like the ship's bows pushing over the surging trees. We broke the ice to fetch the water from the burn and sprawled cosily before the old cast-iron stove at night.

It was an older boys' gang. They were already hillgoers and not just penguins of the piste. They had skied before, some of them, and the rest came tumbling after. A field down by Eggie gave a couple of training days to start – and a hilarious near accident when one novice went shooting off down the edge of the wood just as a pheasant came belting out of it, the two on an unavoidable collision course.

'Och, sur, it's bad enough tryin' tae to keep on ma flippers withoot a pheasant beltin' atween ma legs!'

We did Ben Tirran, 2,860 ft, one day. It was a bit heathery and the weather was grey and lowering. Then it began to snow. It came swirling in down Jock's Road: not violently (you hardly noticed it) but by the time we had cooked chip suppers and were ready for the bed shelf there were six inches on the doorstep. In the morning there were feet of it.

We took to the drifted forests, following up the roads through the bowed and weary greenery, then down in a bliss of fine powder. Quite often the bends were too steep and tight for the beginners and we would see a figure shoot off into space and vanish. There would be a thump and a tree would unload its snow on the victim below.

I provided one spectacular fall by skiing into a tree trunk lying hidden

77

across the road under the snow. The skis had tried to go under while I went over the top. Sore shins, one staved thumb and one broken thumb was the result. Ever tried tying boot laces with two dud thumbs? It was a good excuse for not peeling potatoes though!

After a few days of this rather wild skiing it really started to snow, and blow; the drifts piling up and up. We kept moving our bus, but in the end nothing could be kept clear. Traffic vanished in the glen. The roads were buried. We were cut off.

As we had ample food supplies this did not matter and, having skis, were uniquely mobile – and made the most of it. We skied up to the youth hostel one night, and Dan Smith, hostellers and the farm kids, plus our gang, all squeezed in for a slide show. In the morning we skied down to the phone box at the hotel at Milton, and had to dig down to clear the door so we could get in.

In many places it was possible to ski over gates and fences into fields. All the sheep, cows and horses had escaped and wandered about in search of food. The deer had come down and were pinching the hay, a moorhen sat in a pine tree complaining noisily, and the dog and hares went crazy together, leaving wild tracks in the snow. We met several garrons taking themselves for a walk down the road. It was a period when man and beast alike seemed to lay aside normal fear and enmity.

We dug the telephone box out, reported gleefully, then went on for a good traverse round the valley to marvel at the snow's casual chaos. The plough only got up to Rottal that day. On the next it came up to Milton and on to Braedownie so we eventually worked our way out, driving down canyons of snow higher than the roof.

Dundee's black slushy streets under the glare of street lights seemed a million miles from the white wonderland we had left behind and Fife was clear enough of snow that our story was a bit suspect.

A Remembered Traverse of the Cuillin Ridge

This was written over 20 years ago but I have resisted altering it in any way. Braehead School closed not long afterwards but quite a few of its former pupils still go on the hills, and visit Skye. The Cuillin Ridge must be the 'ultimate day' for Munro-bagging!

W. H. Murray, who has climbed extensively in Scotland, in the Alps and as far as Everest itself, has described the Cuillin Ridge in Skye as 'the longest and grandest day's rock-climbing in Scotland – or elsewhere'.

In the summer of 1967 a party of 14-year-old boys and I did the famous traverse, well called 'the most famous endurance test in the British mountains'. Discussing it afterwards, Murray called this 'a remarkable achievement', which it was, I suppose – though the boys would be scornful of such praise!

It must be the dream of every climber to do the Cuillin Ridge some day, yet, in the 50 years since the first traverse, it has lost little of its stern reputation. It is still a remarkable expedition, unparalleled in Britain.

As Braehead School in Buckhaven has managed more climbing than most schools, Skye has naturally been one of the favourite climbing areas for the experienced. Until this successful traverse, the nearest the school came to success was six years ago. Then Sam, Charlie and Sandy traversed about half the ridge from Sgurr nan Gillean, including climbing down the Basteir Tooth, that fang well seen from the Sligachan Inn. Perhaps the seed was sown then. Three years ago, a former pupil, Joe, a student friend, John, and I tried it – travelling fast as far as the Inaccessible Pinnacle – where we were washed off by a storm. Last year Joe was with me and a school party on the island of Rum, eight miles south of Skye. The Cuillin filled our northern horizon. We had a good party of boys and some of them were with us on new climbs we did at that time. Tom was one. He had climbed in Glen Coe in making a programme for the BBC along with Tom Weir. Billy and Steve were both there. These three then began to dream of the Cuillin Ridge so it was placed on the next summer's programme and they went on 'the short leet' of those who might attempt the traverse.

They began to dig up historical facts. The ridge was first traversed by McLaren and Shadbolt in 1911, thereby ending the dreams of many famous Alpine climbers hoping to be first. T. H. Somervell of Everest fame did the first solo traverse in 1920. In 1939 Charleson and Ford added Blaven as well, and, most remarkable of all, in 1965 it was done in winter conditions by a very strong party: Tom Patey, Hamish McInnes, Brian Robertson and

79

David Crabb, a two-day feat, again a unique British expedition.

From Gars-bheinn to Sgurr na h'Uamha is about ten miles, up and down 10,000 ft over about 38 bumps, most involving some rock-climbing, and at the least giving sensational ridge-walking or scrambling. Sgurr Alasdair, the highest peak, is 3,251 ft and the ridge never drops below 2,500 ft. The mental and physical stamina required is quite enough to deter most people. Many climbers have set off to try it – and failed. To try it with youngsters might well be thought presumptuous; its success, however, was its justification.

Tom, Billy and Steve were well prepared. They had proved competent rock-climbers, their stamina was well tested, they were tough, and morale was high with the school keenly wishing the party well. The responsibility of leading it can be imagined; not that the boys went in ignorance of what was involved. They almost knew the ridge by heart before leaving Fife. I had climbed it all piece-meal many times of course. It was 'simply' a matter of everything clicking into place.

We also had one big traverse in the record – the Mamore Forest – done a few years back, when the same principles were followed: thorough preparation, adequate support parties, food, rest and mental confidence. Four boys did that traverse but the credit was shared by all the dozen involved. Hillary and Tenzing 'only' stood on the Everest team's shoulders.

Apart from one possible element then I do not think any of the party for a minute considered failure. The vital element was weather. Skye has a habit of being too wet to climb, or so hot that it destroys any wish to climb. We chose June as the most hopeful month.

In many ways it was a Himalayan expedition in miniature. We 'sailed' out – school bus to Sligachan; we spent 'weeks' ferrying loads to base – two days for the six miles up Glen Sligachan under Blaven; we reconnoitred and had support parties; lastly, the Traverse Party were left on their own – to succeed or fail alone. 'Logistics' were largely dealt with at school – for example, how many loaves do you need for 13 people for ten days? The answer was about 50. Having a support party for the first part of the ridge meant that we needed food for them going to the starting peak; then they needed food on their own return; and we, the main party, needed food. On the days before the attempt our camp often looked like a grocer's store that had been hit by a hurricane.

We were lucky to have two friends join us: Leon and his son, James. Leon is a doctor – which was also comforting. Another Bill was an old hand and looked after the junior trio: James, Gordon, and Stuart – who were all fairly experienced. A new trio, bigger lads, were less experienced (which nearly caused trouble) but were good carriers: Hugh, Mitch and Eric.

While the 'wee lads' set up camp at Sligachan Hotel, Tom took the others off to carry in hefty loads (food, tents, equipment) to the planned base camp, below Blaven. He managed to get everyone thoroughly lost on the way but in the end managed the job, returning down Glen Sligachan singing in the dark at 2 a.m. At 11 a.m. the site was cleared with five more loads left in the bus. All then carried loads to base. While the tents were pitched and food cooked the other five loads were collected. Those six miles of Glen Sligachan became very familiar. In the end the lads thought nothing of going off on the 12-mile round just to buy some sweets and lemonade at the hotel.

The weather had been roasting. Shirts were dipped in the rivers to try and keep cool. White bodies contrasted with browned arms and legs, for nobody could risk burning shoulders needed for load-carrying.

There was no rest. The next day Leon and Tom set off with a party over the intermediate ridge of Druim Hain to Loch Coruisk in the heart of the encircling Cuillin and from there set up to leave water and food in a cache for the Traverse Party. The heat proved too much and Tom alone managed to make the col below An Stac and leave the vital supplies. It was a grim bit of determined work. I had the other two traversing Clach Glas and Blaven; on the former we did an easy but useful new route, on the latter we tried out the bigger lads to pick the support party – the 'Sherpas' as we called them. Late that night in the tent I picked up a weather forecast. 'The whole of Britain is enjoying a heatwave. This will continue for several days without change.' You could have heard yells of glee in Fife!

'D-Day Minus One' was as hot as ever. Leon, James, Stitch and Stuart set off for the very hard toil up Harta Corrie and Lota Corrie to the Basteir Tooth, to leave vital stove, water and foodstuffs at its foot. We hoped they would make it. We would not know till we got there – if we did. Tom, Bill,

Stob Ban, Mamore Forest

Steve and I set off for Gars-bheinn, the starting peak of the traverse, with Hugh and Mitch the chosen 'Sherpas' who were there to be used as hard carriers and so 'rest' us! Gars-bheinn is 2,934 ft but it took most of the day to reach it. We poured sweat all the way up. There were midges on top! At the highest water we stopped to cook a last proper meal. We also found a deep pool hidden in a rocky cleft, so sticky clothes were soon off for an icy dip.

This was at six in the evening and by eight we had levelled a platform of stones just below the top of the peak. I think we were too excited to sleep much, except Hugh, who snored away happily. The slope ran straight down to the sea with a soft, sweeping view to the Hebrides and Rum. From our eyrie, we heard the faint chug of a boat, the laughter of gulls and a cuckoo – all far, far below. Our bivouac nested among the spires of the Cuillin: peak after peak, rosy in sunset, never untouched by northern glow and, later, moon-washed. This overwhelming experience of beauty alone would have justified the effort. At 11.30 the alarm went off. Porridge and tea took the stiffness out of us. We stood on Gars-bheinn at midnight. Ten minutes later we were off on the experience of a lifetime for any mountaineer.

The rest would be a catalogue but some things we especially recall. The first few peaks, though long and stony, were straight scrambling and passed in a happy daze. It was just like setting out on an Alpine climb: the breath-less quiet of night, the eerie half-light, the crunch of boots on stone, the serrated peaks all about us, the same feeling of unreality . . . the orange moon hidden in a glow of haze. A far lighthouse winked. The stars thickened.

When it became too dark for the ridge's main difficulty just ahead we stopped for another meal. We drank all we could hold from the last natural water we were to see for 12 hours. The Sherpas settled on all six sleeping bags and went to sleep. In the first gleam of day we stole away.

The Sherpas were to have their own private escapade. The first thing we heard on return to base was that Mitch was missing, which, when we heard the story, and even allowing for Mitch's talented thickness, left us wondering just how thick you can be. Nor did Hugh get off without com-ment, from me, and from the rest of the party. They both failed to 'think' which is the first rule of expeditions – as they knew.

A couple of hours after leaving them we yelled across the corrie from Sgurr Alasdair but they were too sound asleep to hear. All they, in fact, had to do was follow a stream from there to the sea and then a cairned path over the ridge to camp, a route Hugh had already done three times. But Mitch stopped for the toilet and Hugh went on – and on – and back to camp, expecting Mitch to be in any minute. He did not arrive. So while we were on the ridge a minor fiasco was going on with the Sherpas. They all turned up in the end but it was a bit embarrassing. That is another story. Back to the Ridge.

Ahead lay the Thearlaich-Dubh Gap, a great rift across the ridge, unavoidable and a serious climbing problem. The rope came out for the climb to it, then quickly everyone abseiled the 40 ft into the gash. The other side rears up for 80 ft and give a 'puff of a climb'. We puffed up it while the light slipped out of the east, setting all the mainland peaks alight above a flood of clouds.

We made a traditional detour off the ridge to climb Sgurr Alasdair, the highest peak in the Cuillin. Exciting situations crowded after each other. It was not difficult, but every step was virtually tip-toed along rooftops hung above walls which fell straight and far into the corries. A slip was unthinkable. About six we were at the foot of An Stac and Tom retrieved the water and food he had hidden. That was a relief. An Stac is another airy climb, straight up several hundred feet of loose ridge, and from the top of its points the famous Inaccessible Pinnacle. Its sides are sheer, so it was like scrambling along a wall with the ground a hundred feet below. The rope came out again for safety. From the top we abseiled off again: 40 feet of sliding down the rope, pushing out from the face of the 'In. Pin.'.

We rested awhile as usual for we were keener to conserve energy than chase records. 'What would we be doing at school just now?' someone asked. We all laughed; we had a normal full day's climbing behind us – and it was still only seven in the morning!

This far we had come before with Joe on the last attempt. It formed a natural third. Ahead lay the testing part – peak after peak and each mountain itself with several rocky towers or knife edges of summits. If we could reach Bruach na Frithe at the end of this (and with the lowest drop of the day just before it), nothing would stop us! We reached it, but how the hours slipped by. It may have only been seven at the Pinnacle: it was 2.30 p.m. by the time we reached the Tooth. The heat of the day; the heat of a heat-wave shimmering off the naked rocks; the heat which had sapped the strength of tough climbers and forced them to give up. Yet the boys did it: patiently, dourly, competently, hour after hour, a lifetime of experience, with still the ready quip and leg-pull, still the unabashed confidence. We cursed the heat – and climbed. As we toiled up Bruach na Frithe we prayed the support party had made the Tooth beyond and left water. We had carefully spun out our half gallon from An Stac, two mouthfuls every other peak. Still there was a spring not far down from the Tooth, so even if the others had failed, with water assured we would do it.

As we dropped to the col at the Tooth we came on the box of supplies. Leon and the boys had done it! (And in fact bagged their Munro.) We drank the half gallon of water straight off and romped down to the spring for more. Then followed tea, and salty beef soup, and more tea and sandwiches with tomatoes and cheese, and lashings of 'Ryvita' and jam. We ate till bursting. We paddled in the pools and threw snowballs at each other. Then, like seals, on the rocks we sprawled out and dreamt a happy hour away. This was the life!

On one of the narrow summits we met a stranded sheep which threatened to dash itself off the crest. We inched forward and eventually it made a rush straight at us, leapt past and stood quivering – and so did we!

At one gap we found a wisp of old snow. We filled our hats and relished the icy fingers of water on our faces. The wind came like the rush of an opening oven and even the brief shadows gave little relief.

Lying on the shadowless rocks eventually roused us and we went back on to the ridge. We left the pools at 2.30 and stood on Sgurr nan Gillean at 5.45. This whole section – the spectacular Basteir Tooth and the West Ridge of Gillean – is again a normal day's climbing. On it we met the only other people that day. They were coming down off Gillean and stood looking after our 'rope' in obvious puzzlement. Not really surprising. By this time practice had brought a fluent efficiency to their technique, whether moving all together or belaying each other over exposed or harder pitches. There was little need to talk, or dither . . . a nod and rope was coiled in, a grunt and a belay was knotted, a word and all moved off as a single unit . . . It must have looked strange; these brown-burnt youngsters moving with the rhythm of a river and smiling quiet greetings as they passed.

Smiling inwardly too, for how could these strangers guess what they had done or what would be over in another five minutes. We scrambled through a window in the ridge and were on the summit of Sgurr nan Gillean.

Now most people have had enough by Gillean and declare that the end of the ridge. However, being dour Braehead types used to doing things thoroughly, our trio demanded (and, I am sure, topographically and morally correctly) to add the last bit of Sgurr na h-Uamha. This peak had sentimental value too; Joe and I had done a new route on it the time we laid the Tooth depôt for the abortive attempt. We uncoiled the rope for the last time to stand on its summit at 7.05 p.m. just under 19 hours from Garsbheinn.

We came down without a pause and this as much as anything demonstrated our fitness. It took just 90 minutes to reach camp by Loch an Athain. At least I did: the trio fell by the wayside – into a favoured pool for half an hour's boisterous fun. I went on to bear the glad tidings.

The next day we had a celebration tea in the Sligachan Hotel. Jellies and cakes and lemonades. It should have been champagne. Everyone, even Hugh and Mitch who gave us an hour of heart failure, had worked together for the success of a day's climbing which will remain fixed in all our experiences as a time of incredible happiness – as is given to few people in this weary world.

It was still a 19-hour day of gruelling climbing; never one to be attempted lightly. Our success, to me, lay in the boys enjoying any and all parts, and no tiredness, no distress marring the conclusion. If it had been a grind ending in exhaustion (as the trip often is) it would have failed. Tom, Bill and Steve instead have a fabulous treasured memory which will last all the days of their lives.

Frosted grasses of winter

The Wanting

I want to walk quiet,
My feet swishing through dewy gale
In a distant glen
Where the budding birches shimmer
Along a busy burn
And an early eagle spins the world
On a wing's turn.

Heaven to me is a curlew morning
In the sun-strong hills.
There stiffened senses can stretch
And the lark-heart soar,
There, some start to salvation,
Away from the claustrophobic world
And its iron-studded doors.

Touch old earth for it yields new dawns.
Laugh like a running child.
No wonder Christ was led to a mountain top
And offered the world free.
I wouldn't have it either, but
It, alas, has me.

AND MORE MUNROS

This time the Munros covered are north and west of the Great Glen and if a certain bias comes through in favour of these remoter parts then I make no apology. West is where the best dreams lie. Having said that, it is the overall quality of the country that steals one's affections. Surprisingly, the areas south of the Great Glen and north of the Great Glen each contribute ten Munros in that compiled list of the Top Twenty. Top it up to the 50, however, and you see the difference . . .

All About Attow

OSLR 33

Beinn Fhada, alias Ben Attow, is a huge elongated sprawl of hill hidden behind the Five Sisters of Kintail and while the latter is made up of several Munros and distinctive minor summits, Ben Attow somehow is left with just the one Munro. Yet few hills are more distinctive, which makes its relative obscurity rather difficult to understand. 'Out of sight, out of mind' probably has a lot to do with it.

Most of Ben Attow comes within the 15,000 acres of the National Trust for Scotland's Kintail property. Fortunately it has been spared the obnoxious developments the NTS have introduced on Ben Lawers or in Glen Coe (quite against the wishes of Percy Unna, whose magnificent gifts of cash for the purchase of mountain lands were made with firm rules about there being no man-made exploitation or development) so Kintail remains the epitome of unspoilt West Highland scenery.

As W. H. Murray says, 'In Kintail everything culminates. Nothing lacks.' The Unna rule of free access at all times makes this splendid area available even during the stalking season, something worth remembering as summer seeks out autumn and the stags start bellowing on the slopes.

Another advantage, particularly in summer, the midges' open season for humans, is the variety of accommodation available in Kintail. There are several hotels and many B-and-Bs scattered round Loch Duich between Dornie and Ratagan. Ratagan also has a pleasant youth hostel, while Shiel Bridge, Morvich and Dornie have camp sites, Glenlicht House is a climbing hut, Camban an open bothy, and Alltbeithe another youth hostel.

Shiel Bridge also has a shop and café, petrol pump and tourist office, there is a restaurant at Ault a' Chruinn, petrol again at Inverinate (a forestry hamlet) and everything at Dornie. Such a variety of services is not common in the West Highlands, so make the most of Kintail, and in the making of it, ensure you visit Ben Attow, that connoisseur's mountain of mountains.

Maybe you should dig out the Ordnance Survey Landranger Sheet 33 if you have not already done so. My copies of this map fall to bits quicker than most – I use it a lot. Annoyingly, the Pathfinder series divides the hill over four sheets (isn't it time the OS produced an Outdoor Leisure map to Kintail?), so we'll stick to the Landranger which will suffice anyway for ordinary walking purposes. From the meeting of rivers west of Attow (Glen Croe) to the meeting of rivers east of Attow (Glen Affric) is a distance of 11 km which certainly makes the Gaelic translation of Beinn Fhada, *long mountain*, an accurate one.

Attow has a magnificent curtain wall above the moat of Gleann Lichd while on the north side are barbicans and bastions and all manner of

Sgurr Mor and Sgurr Beag (Loch Quoich)

cunning defences. The summit area, just to be different, stands on the edge of one of the most extensive high plateaux in Scotland; certainly there is nothing like it, apart from Ben Alder, outwith the Cairngorms. For all this, the hill can still be ascended 'with hands in pockets'.

Start the day at Dorusduain or Morvich. There is more parking space at the former and, below the house, a bridge leads across to join the Morvich-Gleann Choinneachain path. This path pulls up steadily, squeezed between the steep flanks of our hill and the deeply seamed slopes of A' Ghlas bheinn, with the vocal river 'makin musik' between. There are several falls.

The path crosses the stream that drains the slabby dual corries to the south and, after a smaller burn, puts in some zigzags to gain height and win the corridor of the Bealach an Sgairne. Sometimes the path doubles as a burn but it is a well-made one nevertheless.

The bealach is worth visiting. Sometimes called the 'Gates of Affric', it is all a pass should be and a very old east-west route. Loch Duich is named after St Duthac and he came over the pass in the eleventh century. The path beyond drops to Loch a' Bhealaich which seems to be at the head of Affric but in fact drains north to Glen Elchaig, its waters the main supply for the mighty spout of the Falls of Glomach.

Gleann Gniomhaidh, over a vague, peaty watershed, is the true upper end of Glen Affric (north branch), a rather wet and bleak glen. Years ago we had to leap a peaty cutting while descending the glen and the last person caught his toe on a tussock just as he took off and did a gold-medal dive into the black ooze. We thought it very funny but he refused to give us an encore.

One of the great walks is not up Attow but round it, crossing the Bealach an Sgairne and returning round and down Gleann Lichd: not an easy option but a superb alternative. Our day is a compromise to take in the summit and some of this circuit. Having viewed the Promised Land of Affric, return west again.

At the top of the zigzag up Gleann Choinneachan there is a side path with a cairn at the start (but not shown on the OS map) which wends up Coire an Sgairne and gains the col between Meall a' Bhealaich and the summit plateau. This is our route, one which makes big Ben Attow a very easy ascent for all its size. A steady plod leads up to the trig point: 1,032 metres, Munro No. 97. Of the 277 Munros, 135 are over the 1,000-metre mark, so Attow is quite well up in the list.

The huge slope to the west is the Plaide Mhor (the big plaid) and an interesting but slightly tricky return to Loch Duich can be made by crossing it to the Sgurr a'Choire Ghairbh ridge and down by Beinn Bhuidhe. *The peak of the rough corrie*, which lies beyond *the hunters' col*, hints at potential problems and there are some tricky spots requiring scrambling up wee slabs or crags. There are endless bumps on the tortuous ridge.

This is the high, crenellated crest you see from the A87 causeway – which is maybe another reason fewer walkers head for Attow. They think it is all like that! The tidy Munroist who is also climbing Tops will have to go across to the first bump, Meall an Fhuarain Mhoir, *hill of the big well*. A second Top lies the same distance from the summit but in the opposite direction, which is the way I suggest you continue the walk.

This takes us along the rim of the NE corrie, a lonely spot, loud with stags' roaring in the autumn, and with fine views over to Sgurr nan Ceathreamhnan. South lies the Five Sisters are Beinn Mhor (*big hill* as against our *long hill*) and you also look out to the glitter of the western sea – something which makes climbing in the west incomparable.

Beyond the top of Sgurr a' Dhubh Doire (*peak of the black wood*), which looks, and is, quite a sharp peak in the view along Glen Affric there are still 4 km of ridge running down into Glen Affric but you can turn down equally well to Camban. The Scottish Mountaineering Club Western Highlands district guide admits that a traverse of Attow like this is 'a very fine expedition' – so it must be good.

With the variety of accommodation available, one could enjoy staying out beyond Ben Attow for a night, at Camban bothy or Alltbeithe youth hostel, returning the next day. Travelling without a tent in summer should not make too heavy a pack, even for the traverse of Ben Attow.

The return to base is as fine a pass as Attow is a ben. Once over the watershed the scenery becomes grand. I've heard it called Himalayan, quite a fair comparison. There is a section of gorge with trailing falls, then the path descends steadily to the long flat strath with Glenlicht House at its head. This is a 'hut' belonging to Edinburgh University Mountaineering Club.

The tired legs of evening can find level Gleann Lichd as hard as a morning hill. On a day as long as this I'd make sure my party carried a stove and dixie. A brew stop in a fine setting is one of the great joys of the mountains, along with dipping hot, sweaty feet or bodies in a cooling stream – preferably downstream of the water source for the brew!

I've seen us cowering in the open cellar at the gable of Glenlicht House while the wind and wet yowled outside (and we filled the shelter with our body steam) – a very lifesaver of a brew that one. Ben Attow, unless you are experienced, is strictly a walk for a good summer's day. A winter traverse really is a bit Himalayan.

About 1 km along the glen from the hut, a stream descends the wall of Ben Attow from a tiny lochan, Loch Chuirn Deirg. For years this odd-looking feature fascinated me and I intended to go up and see if there really was a lochan in such an improbable spot. But the way up is hard work and sloth prevailed for long enough. However, if a ploy seems daft enough, it becomes much more attractive. In the end I went up alone in midwinter and camped by the lochan. It does exist.

The ascent was made harder by a good covering of soft snow and by eating a haggis supper at the car before setting off! The theory of this move was that if I ate first and climbed afterwards there would be less weight to carry. Unfortunately the meal weighed more inside my tummy that it would have done inside my rucksack. We live and learn.

The lochan is a tiny one, set like a navel in a bellyfold of the obese mountain and an entertaining camp site. Several places, on the Five Sisters ridge or on the path up Beinn Bhuide above Croe Bridge, have the same sort of feature with, or without, water filling the hollow left by the contorted schisty strata.

One abiding memory of that high camp was the interminable length of the December night: dark at 4 p.m. and only light again at 8 a.m. Tape, book and candle helped pass the hours before sleeping. Maybe plenty of time influenced my choice of tapes – Mahler's 6th symphony – played through three times.

The book was one of Lea McNally's about red deer which I read just once. These both seemed appropriate in the setting; the candles I suppose could have doubled as emergency rations. As I'm never allowed to spend 12 hours in bed normally, the truth was I really enjoyed my long night on the long mountain.

Glen Pean Cottage

The air thickens
In the deserted glen,
Only the dusk moves.
I sit out
Under ash,
Under a black crag, the hillside red
With day closed, only the faint stirring
Of dusk wind to remind of time.
The night stars me
With silence,
Broken only by mousy murmurings
Of water –
Prayers, tip-toe-touching into
The schisty cathedrals of our hearts.
I sit long with silence,
I sleep sound, under crossed rafters,
Under moonlight resurrection,
Postponing forever
If I could
The return south.
Death would be easy in this quiet place . . .
It was life that proved intolerable.
My grandfather's grandfather fled it
To cross oceans of exile
But I return
For a single night,
A solitary dusk
The homeless home
With the balm of silence.

Seeds grow from silence
And cold stone
May be warmed into
Life again.

Rock textures on the Kilfinnan Burn

Mull: Easter on the Heights
OSLR 48

'Where do you want off?' the driver asked as we sped down Glen More in the Iona Ferry bus from Craignure.

'At the bridge, please' – but I should have said 'right now', for framed in the glen was the bold, angular bulk of Ben More of Mull, sovereign Munro in all the isles (other than extravagant Skye). The hill lay sharp as an oil painting, very clear, a blaze of blue beyond, a picture which might never come our way again.

We were dropped off at the bridge (after a wee chat, for on Mull bus drivers are still people) and he said the weather might last, even if they'd 'used up half the annual good days this one week'.

The bus had picked us up in eastern Glen More where we had left the car for our exit from the hills once we had given Colin his first Munro and I had climbed my penultimate Corbett of the revised listings. Not that Mull or Ben More need such meagre reasons for a visit. As one of the finest walking areas anywhere with some magnificent through-routes for the gangrel, Mull does not need 'listed' summits.

As the bus sped off for Loch Scridain and the Ross of Mull, we were panting up the Brideag Burn, thankful to be going over only the first bosses of hill to pitch camp near where I had first camped on the island a score of years before. That, too, had been during an Easter heatwave, with a school group, while now the sun smote down on a young nephew. The heat was tempered by mercy, however, as, despite the sun, a bitter wind blew. For walking it was an unusual perfection: no rain, no midges, no sweat.

The slopes were deep-littered in tawny grass which we collected in armfuls to place under the ground sheets. Boulders from the burn provided stools. We brewed, and with the tea we ate the last of the Christmas cake. Migrant wheatears flew past the site. A first wood anemone was in flower in a rocky nook above a deep pool of startling clarity.

I recounted to Colin how, on that first visit, everyone dived and splashed in the water and then wandered slowly upstream from tempting pool to delectable waterfall, to better pool. My snooze by the tents had been broken an hour or two later by shouts and yells as down the hillside came what looked like a gang of naked savages. The slopes were just sprouting new growth after extensive burning and proved very sharp to bare feet, hence the war dances. They were also sending up clouds of black soot. A good excuse for another swim. Our ascent of Ben More on that first visit was via the head of the glen, then over A'Chioch: hot, grim work and we ended up on top, quivering like the view.

We also had an unforgettable encounter with island midges. The sweltering day had brought them to the boil and, as we were dependent on public transport and were camping, flight was impossible. We camped on a breezy knoll above a burn on the slopes of Ben More, saved largely by anabatic and catabatic winds. The cleft of the burn was windless and held a seething stew of midges. One could reach an arm into the buzz and, in a second, it would be covered in a black, tactile skin of insects. Draw the arm out again and they fell off like blowing coal dust. It was a shivery fascination to do this for at the back of one's mind was the vision of doom if the kindly breezes should go. On that visit, however, the breeze sent for reinforcements and a gale drove us to Tobermory youth hostel, an eighteenth-century building overlooking the bay. At the storm's climax we went to Calgary Bay to see immense rollers smashing ashore, spray flying inland for hundreds of yards, and the waterfalls standing on end. Today's ascent with Colin would be quite different.

Ben More is a big tent-shaped block from many angles, with the lower cone of A' Chioch lying to the east. The hill often looks black and forbidding, for the rock is mainly basalt and forms a decaying heap with great skirts of scree. This is not to denigrate it. Loch na Keal or Loch Scridain, the usual starting points, are sea lochs. You climb all its 3,169 ft (966 metres). The hard work is rewarded by hauling out as fine a hill view as you'll enjoy in Britain, ranging from Ireland in the south to the Torridons in the north, and with the Outer Hebrides down the western horizon. Cuillin, Rum, Ardgour, Nevis, Etive, Cruachan, Arran, Jura, all these and other mainland or island hills will be displayed – assuming there is anything to see at all. Ben More is a favourite, perhaps the top favourite, of all Munros that are kept for 'the last' by those who have been ticking off the list.

The next favourite is the Inaccessible Pinnacle – being 'the hardest Munro' may contribute to its selection (or exclusion) – but Ben More is kept for the last for geographical reasons and, I'm sure, a touch of the romantic. Being on an island does mean a certain extra organisation is required in reaching it, so Ben More is often only given consideration well on in a walker's Munro-ing, at which stage the thought is planted 'This would be a splendid Munro to finish on.' Oddly, it was my first Munro when I set off to do all the Munros in a single expedition. That was a heatwave April as well, with the girls in bikinis, and regretting it by the return to our camp by Loch Scridain. They were all too literally 'in the pink' by then.

I have just checked my record for weather in case I'm also conveying the idea that the weather in Mull is always sunny. I find notes of ascents with 'traverse in thick mist', 'severe gales', 'miserable conditions', 'thick, wet clag', so the weather is fairly average. But when it is good, it is very, very good.

Colin and I cut the corner a bit before the head of the valley as we wanted to follow up a side-stream descending from the pap of A'Chioch – water would be welcome up high with such thirsty walking. Hills began rising all round. Mull is surprisingly hilly and feels big enough that you can forget you are on an island.

I'm sure the majority of the people who climb Ben More plod up from Dishig. A pity, for the finest approach is undoubtedly the ridge from

A'Chioch. I'd recommend our line from Glen More, or by Glen Clachaig from Loch Ba, and these also combine for a fine through route. A'Chioch is a cone of 'chaotic rubbish' to quote one of my lads, but any traverse to avoid the bump is probably worse. Once on the ridge to Ben More the going becomes more interesting. We followed a white hare to begin with, Storm tracking it along the edge of nothing in a way we found rather nerve-wracking on a sort of Carn Mor Dearg Arête type of ridge. Ben More's north face was still deeply snow covered, scarred by fallen cornices, and the rocks crowning it were grey-bearded with overnight frost.

We could hear voices above us and Storm shot off to bark insults at the trespassers. A couple from Derbyshire and a lad from Edinburgh exchanged greetings and exclamations of delight. Storm rolled on the snow. Colin ate an Easter egg. We stayed on top for half an hour. By then, another man and dog had arrived and a Croydon school party was approaching.

Those who have kept Ben More for their last Munro will be delighted at the choice – assuming the day is fair for Ben More has a bad-weather hazard shared with the Skye Munros: its summit rocks are magnetic and the compass reads inaccurately. This is quite amusing (or quite alarming) for we are so brainwashed into believing 'the compass never lies' that the resulting chaos when it does lie is beyond understanding. A careful bearing off the summit of Ben More will take you down on a quite unscheduled line! A party, having taken a careful bearing and popping out under the cloud to find the 'wrong' prospect below, is somewhat disconcerted. You have been warned!

The effect is only bad on the summit. Knowing this in advance, one just takes care on arrival and there are well-defined ridges and corrie edges which help one to navigate effectively. The map alone has to be the aid leaving the summit. A trick I learnt for Skye conditions was to make tiny (two pebbles) cairns up the last bit. Then the way off was clear and the markers were easily enough kicked over in passing during the descent.

We scampered off, along to the A'Chioch col, then down into Coir' Odhar and over to follow the ridge rather than the valley back to the tents. We managed to stalk five hinds to about 50 yards and, shortly afterwards, Storm set up two hares which careered off to panic another group of hinds. For a while the whole hillside seemed to be moving.

We found some big whalebacks of rough gabbro, but they were too easy-angled to be of scrambling interest. The basalt is useless, too, and the red granites of Fionnphort are too small. Mull is not a rock climbers' island. We arrived back at the tents ready for a brew and all too soon the shadows crept down. I kept moving up the hillside with my book to stay in the sun. The day grew bitterly cold, and after supper we burrowed into our sleeping bags.

Mull has some superb trekking routes and the next day we had a good sample. As we'd be motoring that way later, we hid the tents and other odds and ends beside the next burn up Glen More, hiding them with the plentiful grass. The river came down in many little falls and the old path was visible only occasionally as we sweated up Coir a'Mhaim. (Many old paths in Mull are no longer maintained.) There was a long levelling-out

Rock colours in the Shiants

with the burn slowly shrinking till it vanished and we were on the Mam Breapadail.

There was no gentle watershed crossing: the ground fell away into Coire Mor with Devil's Beef Tub steepness and Glen Cannel seemed miles below, yet we were soon down to brew where several streams joined, each draining an equally fine corrie, an impressive heart to the mountains of Mull. A purply haze crept over the ridges and only when we smelled it did we realise it was burning. The shepherds were busy using the dry spell.

A mile down the glen was a ruined farm, while, across the valley, lay long-abandoned burial grounds – the 'dead centre of Mull' Colin reckoned. People no longer live in these remote spots; the shepherds come in by Land Rover and return to comfy homes on the coast at night. The gain is sometimes ours as we acquire a bothy here and there. We headed up to one now.

On the way, we passed a 'bird-cone' which had been much used by a buzzard for it was well whitewashed and surrounded by animal skulls, vertebrae, fluff and feathers. These cones seem to be a phenomenon peculiar to the islands. Usually they are coastal, but here they were central and in profusion. A slight knoll makes a perch, the birds' droppings encourage growth, dust is caught by the growth and the process builds up a solid green cone. On Jura I have seen them five feet high.

Glen Forsa was busy with men and dogs driving sheep, so after the statutory brew Colin, Storm and I headed up Glen Lean for Beinn Talaidh (Talla on some maps). We more or less kept to the stream itself – 'burning up' – till, near the top, the burn ran in a small gorge so there might even be some scrambling. Almost at valley level we had found some aluminium rods and I hoped it might be parts of a meteorological balloon, but after finding some other bits we realised there had been a plane crash somewhere nearby.

The pieces of wreckage became steadily more numerous as we boulder-hopped up the burn with bits of complicated machinery appearing as well as the mangled bits of the aircraft's skin. A big strut lay on the bank. Then ahead we saw a pile of grey – as if a lorry had tipped a load of rubbish into the gorge.

There must have been mice living in the wreckage, for Storm was soon all but invisible – just his tail waving from a jagged hole. There was a propeller showing and one big and one small wheel. We thought we saw two engines, but it was all so broken up it was difficult to recognise anything. One 'sliding part' was made of stainless steel and glittered with surprising freshness. Much of the wreckage was thoroughly embedded in the rocky banks.

We climbed on, but the walls had converged to a narrow gut down which shot the small, but wetting stream. The alternative was an ungardened Jericho Wall. We scrambled up a loose-enough exit line. Storm rushed off and was soon tail-flag-waving in another hole. It looked like a rabbits' burrow, but this was 1,700 ft up and all we saw were hares in various stages of change from winter to summer colouring. There are either high-level rabbits on Mull or hares that burrow.

The east flank of Talaidh is steep so any distraction was welcome. Eventually we came up against the summit screes, but just as we were about to tackle them I noted a faint track going off at a slant to the right. Whether it was made by man, sheep or deer, we did not debate. We used it thankfully, crossed a rim of snow and were soon tramping up the final shales of Beinn Talaidh, a splendid Corbett.

The glory had departed: steely greys and denim blues filled in the picture, like a poster done by a child with a limited range of felt-tipped pens. But we reckoned that, as a viewpoint, it was superior to Ben More. This is very often true of many Corbetts and lesser summits. They may not be up to much in themselves, but they can provide far better grandstands than their nearby big brothers.

Dun da Gaoithe is Mull's other Corbett and it stands in the eastern block. It can be climbed in a pleasant circuit from Craignure or by taking the Iona bus round to Glen More and returning over the Corbett. There are several other good hills, such as Ben Buie, which lie south of the Glen More road and, perhaps as rewarding as any ascent, the through-glens, bealachs, and coastal paths give as rich a variety of lower walks as you'll find anywhere – the irrationally neglected aspect of Mull. Lochbuie, with its ancient stone circle, clan keep and remoteness, is a fascinating place. Its post office is one of the smallest in Britain. Loch Spelve with its many arms is seldom visited. In some ways one wants a boat for Mull as well. One of my friends actually kept Ben More as his last Munro simply so he could sail to the island.

The longer you have on Mull, the better the return on the financial investment of the journey. The Oban-Craignure vehicle ferry is not cheap, the Fishnish-Lochaline ferry, while considerably cheaper, lands one in Morven which is a long way away if you are coming from the south so, if you are paying for the crossing, it pays to stay. Once or twice I've got round this problem by taking a push-bike to Mull or just going on foot and using public transport. Services are only fully operational in summer and a practical drawback then is the lack of beds on the island, especially since walkers and climbers in particular don't want to be pinned-down to pre-booking everything. Camping is an alternative but, if combined with midges and the rain, can land one in a psychiatric ward.

Colin and I did not face such considerations on top of Talaidh. Our study of the view was cut short by a flurry of snow. We scuttled off down the long north ridge. The whole of Glen Cannel seemed to be in flames with arcs of fire zipping up the hills and rolling great clouds of smoke into the air. Looked at from lower down, it seemed like the setting for some epic film. Red deer pranced around in obvious distrust of this strange, fiery world. Thankfully our transverse glen had not been set alight. We cooked our bothy supper with the fires in front and behind flickering and dying and flaring up again. Even after dark the gold eyes of the blaze glanced along the slopes of Glen Forsa.

Frequent notes in the bothy book mentioned the crashed aircraft. One writer said he had turned down a lift on that very flight while stationed in Iceland. The crash date was 1 February 1945 and the plane was on a Canada-Prestwick flight. When we went into the church hall in Salen two days later, a framed citation told us a few more details. Surprisingly, there had been five survivors. Their flashing lights had been seen and local rescue set out in 'the worst conditions in living memory'. Dr Flora MacDonald was given an MBE, there were three BEM's awarded and various other commendations.

The bothy book also had many entries complaining about heat. 'The guide says Mull is one of the wettest of islands. Rubbish!' I wonder if that writer stayed on the island long enough to realise the guide's veracity. I can only think most of the visitors came to Mull *because* the weather was good. Sadly, most entries also pointed out the brief nature of visits: the minimum required to grab Ben More.

When I looked out of the skylight in the morning, it was to discover that the meteorological fire brigade had arrived in the night and dampened down everything. We rose to exit while the rain held off. Only under the slopes of Beinn Bheag, Talaidh's lesser neighbour, did we discover that both sides of Glen Forsa had been fired. Our boots were soon black and messy while the dog's underparts were many times worse. At one stage he slipped and covered his face in clinging black soot.

We washed him once we ran out of the burnt area and just made the car in Glen More before the rain came on. No matter how many days of good weather you may have on Mull, it is still one of the wettest islands in the west. I hope one day Colin will realise how lucky he was.

A buzzard flew up from a wayside telegraph pole. The island seems to have scores of the birds and we wondered where they perched before man erected these uprights. We drove up over the pass through boiling cloud. The rain eased. Then we saw where the early smoke of yesterday had come from. All the flanks of western Glen More were black. I groaned. Somewhere up there lay our cache of tents and other odds and ends. As we approached we could see some of the items peering through the black fur of burnt grass. The Ultimate Tramp tent was melted into a lump of green goo and the gas cartridges had no doubt added their contribution to the conflagration but, when ready to weep, under it all, unharmed, we found my obsolete Challis tent. I would have sacrificed a dozen others for it – my friend of the months of the Munros-in-one trip, of part of the Groat's End Walk, of visits to Atlas and Arctic and to the Nanda Devi Sanctuary! Colin probably thought my glee most irrational.

There was no view of Ben More. As we were loading the car the Iona Ferry bus drew up. The driver asked if we had had a good trip.

'Great, just great,' we replied.

He looked at the wall of rain sweeping up Loch Scridain. But that was nothing to some I've met on Mull. The worst night ever in a 'camper' for instance. Parked on the Ross of Mull, I had to hold my supper pan on the cooker (gimbals are not part of a camping car's standard equipment) and I hardly slept as I feared the van was going to be blown over. If you must have it bad there is a certain satisfaction in having it memorably so.

But my memories of Mull are many and varied: Duart Castle in a day of deep summer blue, the sunset bonfire by Loch Scridain at the start of my walk over all the Munros. Glen More echoing to the curdling cries of curlews, the *Captain Scott*'s anchor dragging in Tobermory Bay in the middle of the night, a ceilidh in the pub at Salen after we'd walked across the island . . . To me, these are all part of the joys of being in the mountains, or on an island. On Mull you have the best of several worlds – usually.

In Search of a Maiden

OSLR 19

Where were you on Midsummer Day 1992? Up a Munro maybe for this was the day of the *Boots* attempt at doing all the Munros at the same hour. It must have been one of the busiest days on the hills in years, or the busiest weekend, for some Munros are easier done with the help of an intermediate camp or bothy, especially in the north and west of Scotland.

These remote areas tend to be left unvisited till well on in one's Munro-bagging history. Once past the 200-up they all seem to be in awkward places! Awkward is a relative term and what it means is a break in the normal complete dependence on cars which is causing immense harm to the pastime of Munro-bagging. But that is another story. Let me keep to the awkwardness of A'Mheaghdean and, in particular, our visit to it on *Boots 92*.

At our midgy camp by Loch Maree we heard the weekend forecast: Scotland would be hot and sunny except for the north and west where conditions would be cloudy with the possibility of rain at times. We could not kid ourselves we were other than north-west and the clouds were verifying the forecast with marked determination. Why, oh why, had I picked A'Mhaighdean, regarded as the remotest Munro, for the one to climb on the *Boots Across Scotland* event?

The answer of course was that for something so special I wanted a special hill. A'Mhaighdean (*the Maiden*) is a 'coy bitch' as I once heard her described. 'Not easy to pick up.' The hill stands in that wild country north of Loch Maree, moated by lochs and rough miles, a real macho, male landscape. Even experienced hillgoers feel like fumbling adolescents faced with that bared beauty.

Midsummer day though? That would be different. Little darkness. Blazing sun maybe. Why not canoe over and slip through for a bivvy on the summit itself, with an incomparable viewpoint to top and tail the day? My partner in crime had not canoed before. After five minutes afloat she turned turtle. After seven minutes she did so again. After ten minutes she decided walking was advisable. Being in Morocco, I missed this experimental session so it came about that we two and her dog, Joss, set off to hoof it in to Lochan Fada. We would camp there and fight the bogs to the Munro for the 1–2 p.m. *Boots* deadline on the summit, return to camp, then out and home next day. Why are forecasts always right when the forecast is bad?

What is *Boots* all about? Over the years there have been many attempts

From the top of A'Mhaighdean looking to Beinn Lair, etc.

to climb all the Munros on the same day, usually involving teams doing huge days with inadequate manpower. None has ever succeeded. In May 1988 the first *Boots* tried to have someone on top of all the Munros simultaneously and enrolled about 2,000 people, often with summits covered by more than one party. It nearly succeeded. The day before was brilliant, the day after the event was superb, the day of the event was diabolical. However, it was not just a record-seeking gimmick but an event which set out to raise money for a cause which itself struck a chord with a whole range of hillgoers, partly I think, because when we hear of accidents there is the thought 'There, but for grace, goes I.' Hillgoers are fierce in their freedoms and so feel deeply for any kindred spirit who falls foul of the hills.

Big Davy Pearson was one such. After a horrendous fall down the Trilleachan Slabs he was lucky to be alive, but had been brain-damaged and confined to a wheelchair. He owed his life to the Glen Coe Mountain Rescue Team and Stobhill Hospital – and all three were seen as worthy of support by Gordon Pearson, who had the idea of a sponsored Munro bash to raise money. May 1988 was chosen.

A nephew, Colin, and I canoed down Loch Ericht on that occasion and climbed Beinn Bheoil from our base at Ben Alder bothy. Both visibility and temperature were about zero on the summit. It was a shame, except the initial target of £20,000 was left behind and a grand £75,000 rolled in. Since then scores of disadvantaged people and worthy mountain causes (particularly in the field of safety and rescue) have been assisted. Can you imagine how a blind girl feels when she stands on top of Ben Nevis with the wind and sun on her face?

One spin-off has been a series of entertaining yet important safety lectures by the guide Mick Tighe. I was lucky to make the evening at Glenrothes, and most enjoyable it was. This is one of the secrets of *Boots* I feel: it touches everyone. It is utterly non-elitist. About the good news of the hills. Over 3,000 people have attended these lectures, have learnt and will pass on what they learnt. A lot of boots to stand on the magic Munros – safely.

On our *Boots* bash Val, Joss and I headed off from Incheril, along by Loch Maree and (good paths always) up Gleann Bianasdail in what Scots would term 'gey dreich' conditions. And that was the best of the weather over the vital weekend. Unlike 1988, however, it was not universal. South of the Great Glen the days were hot, sunny, and marvellously clear. We pitched on a rare patch of grass near the river's outflow from Lochan Fada, a site shared by goats and passing *Boots* folk. We hoped there would be wind enough to keep the midges away but not enough to blow the tent away. The midges there are man-eaters, woman-eaters, dog-eaters . . .

At 6 p.m. the drizzle was driving past. We slept. At 6 a.m. the drizzle was still driving past. The bogs, dry for weeks, were happily mopping up the wet. After an hour along the south shore of the loch our feet had mopped up a ration of wet too. Val complained that 'lochan' was supposed to mean a *small* loch. Lochan Fada could be sued under the Trades Description Act she reckoned. A trace of track along the red rock strata (*c.* 350-metre level), bits of goat path and steady tramping took us to the far end, a shoreline without a tideline of plastic rubbish for once. Wedged between the great cliffs of Beinn Lair and the jumbled mass of A'Mhaighdean we sat eating our 'pieces' (sandwiches) in as remote a corner as you could find in Scotland. Pity we couldn't see anything above the 1,000 ft tideline of cloud. Or maybe it was as well. The contours couldn't have been closer for the initial pull up on to Beinn Tharsuinn Chaoil, A'Mhaighdean's outer defences, but we seemed to drift up effortlessly.

We had been too efficient and had to slow down. We 'slittered' up the mountain in the end. Val learnt the names of some of the bright alpine flowers which grew, 'with their heads down', at Munro altitude: thrift, campion, cyphel, thyme, ladies' alpine mantle, club mosses and the like. We procrastinated over lunch in the lee of a boulder and through the mist loomed a Fife trio who were also putting the *Boots* in on the Maiden. (Wherever possible an additional party went up each Munro – just to make sure.)

One of the joys of Scottish hillgoing is the camaraderie that exists. Even here we found these Fifers were from Freuchie and two nights before had been in the pub with the lad who had sold Val her dog. Several of our local club were out too and my nephew, Colin, this time was off on Mull with a friend. I hoped Ben More was kind to them. Connections. Wear a *Boots* T-shirt and thousands will hail you as mate.

A'Mhaighdean's summit is a superlative viewpoint. Val took my word for it. Visibility was about 50 yards. Ah well, that's the way the quartzite crumbles! We groped our way over to bag Ruadh Stac Mor as well and met its *Boots* gang tiptoeing down its rufous screes.

Val and I had a second lunch in a boulder howff (shelter) on the col. This howff was a life-saver on a day of blizzards when I was doing the round of the six peaks and became caught there instead of making an exit to Corriehallie as I half intended. That was my excuse anyway. As I carried everything I needed to camp-out, the sight of the howff was irresistible. I just had to have a night there. That a blizzard blew up was coincidence. There is something smug about lying cosy in a sleeping bag with the snow blasting past only inches away – especially when there is no window in between! A'Mhaighdean was an Ice Maiden on that visit.

As it was on my first ever (winter) visit in 1964 during a Hogmanay stay at Torridon's Ling Hut. A friend with the only car ran me up to the Heights of Kinlochewe where I slept in the stable and tramped up to Lochan Fada the next day. The lochan was frozen solid and made a ridiculously easy highway. (I just regretted not having skates with me!) Not so easy was the long walk 'home' again to the Ling Hut: a moonlit night of scudding clouds and the road flowing with spindrift. A massive but magical day.

In the *Boots* conditions we were glad of a shorter walk 'home', to the tent angling along and down under Beinn Tarsuinn to the other end of Lochan Fada (wondering how many folk had even walked both its end shores on the same day), chatting to other participants, passing where the Freuchie lads had camped, and rejoining our neighbourhood goats in the gorge: 6 p.m. and the drizzle was blasting past the tent. Why are the forecasts always right when you want them to be wrong? Wouldn't it be nice if we actually had a climate in Scotland instead of a ragbag of weather?

South of the Great Glen it was marvellous weather, however. We saw that when we headed home the next day, completing our 500 miles of motoring for the chosen Munro. We were glad it was clear elsewhere. On Mullach Clach a'Bhlair there was a very special gathering, thanks to the landowner, a good driver and willing friends. Big Davy (could he ever have dreamt what a world of pleasure his misfortune has led to?), a girl with ME, a girl with motor-neurone disease and a man with no legs all made the Munro. The last played his fiddle and the company had a dance! A boy with spina bifida went up on his pony.

Our *Boots* route could well be the easiest option for those just after A'Mhaighdean or it in conjunction with Ruadh Stac Mor, even as a day outing. An alternative descent could be made by the Heights of Kinlochewe (Gleann na Muice) though this gives a deal of walking on estate roads rather than stalkers' paths. The approach from the north invariably means staying overnight at Shenaval bothy which is often overcrowded and still a long way from the Munro. Carnmore, from the west (Kernsary), is also an option. Being prime stalking country, late summer/autumn is best avoided, a modest return for our freedom to roam at other times. And the landowner has resisted the easy option of bulldozing tracks through this landscape. He thinks it very special too.

The steep contours and cliff signs round A'Mhaighdean and its neighbours should be noted. This is perhaps the wildest and most dramatic corner of mainland Britain. Even where the map looks simple the ground can be bare, slabby rock and endless bumps and hollows, all beyond map delineation but giving a severe test of navigation confidence, and competence, in poor visibility. We found that on the *Boots* visit when, even with nine previous visits, I felt under pressure. Watch the Maiden! It is a good hill to keep for a Midsummer day visit – but do have a word with the weather man first.

Though the second *Boots Across Scotland* event has passed, the good work it makes possible continues unobtrusively from year to year. Donations are still welcomed, new members are welcomed (a newsletter keeps everyone up to date) and new volunteers are needed for when the next attempt comes round. Perhaps your area is suitable for a safety lecture? Perhaps you know disabled folk who could be helped through *Boots*. For any of these reasons, do please get in touch (and keep in touch) by writing to the secretary, R. McWilliam, Pleanbank Farmhouse, Plean, Stirlingshire. Tel: 0786–816412. Make any donations out to *Boots Across Scotland*.

Loch Ericht: Munro-bagging by canoe, 'Boots Across Scotland 1988'

Wyvis – Hill of Terror

OSLR 20

Motorists swooping down to Inverness after driving north up the A9 are often aware of a vast sprawl of mountain filling the view beyond the Beauly Firth and the Black Isle. This is Ben Wyvis, which stands in splendid isolation between Wester and Easter Ross. It has its toes in the eastern sea but its eyes watch sunsets over far western peaks.

The hill has never been oversubscribed, its rights issue largely being taken up by those with a large portfolio of Munros. The prospectus that so catches the eye from the A9 somehow vanishes when one nears the mountain. As the traveller heads up the Cromarty Firth Wyvis simply disappears behind its subsidiary summits. Turning off on the Ullapool road beyond Garve Wyvis is too near so it is just a featureless mass which is also rapidly being taken over by maturing spruce. Yet this is the side from which one normally makes a bid for Wyvis.

Garbat is clearly shown on the Landranger map and there is a large carpark. The trouble with plantations is the way they change the basic landscape and then keep altering it in detail: a new bulldozed track here, an extension to the plantings there – and none of it on the map. So don't blame anyone if there are surprises on Wyvis.

Though an easy hill in good conditions, it can be challenging when the cloud comes down or big winds blow. A hill which simply goes to a sharp point gives simple navigation; a sprawling plateau like Wyvis can land one with post-graduate tests in navigation. So keep Wyvis for a clear day.

Going up Wyvis on a clear day is also recommended for a positive reason – the big reward of the ascent is the tremendous panoramic view from the summit plateau, the result of the hill's isolated position as the only giant in the east. One can recognise peaks away up in Caithness or down in the Cairngorms (often blue toned as their name) while, from Affric to Torridon to An Tealach, there is an immense array of peaks and ridges. You actually see the ice-worn, bitten-plateau world that is the Highlands. Given a temperature inversion, the white clouds filling the valleys can look just like glaciers flowing between mountains.

The summit plateau of Wyvis is an unusually soft mossy spread (on schisty rock) which gives walking the sensation of having a carpet with a deep pile underfoot. One Munroist, keeping Ben Wyvis for his 'last', took his golf clubs up and played himself in, holing out on Glas Leathad Mor (*the big grey slope*) as the 1,046-metre highest point is called. This soft vegetation would be quickly eroded were any mechanical ski development allowed but for the odd ski-tourer the hill offers excellent activity though even that depends on conditions. A sleeping lion is still a dangerous creature.

When Martin Moran was doing his winter Munros expedition he and his wife climbed Wyvis and, while skiing along the plateau in storm conditions, they drifted on to an eastern cornice which then triggered a huge avalanche and swept them hundreds of feet down the mountain. They were unharmed. Two months later a lone skier was killed in an avalanche on Wyvis. The hill, pronounced *Wivis* or, locally, *Weevis* (never *Wye-vis*), probably means *mountain of terror*!

On a clear summer's day the hill offers a steep but easy ascent. Walk along the A835 to follow up the Allt a'Bhealaich Mhoir (*burn of the big pass* – separating Wyvis from Little Wyvis) and on to the end spur of An Cabar. Or enter the forest at Garbat and follow the forestry track, then a path, to the top of the forest and wander up past the experimental high plot. The walk on to the trig point is a grand highway. Whichever way up was taken, use the other in descent or, if wanting to make a day of it, continue on over Tom a'Choinnich, Carn Gorm, Meallan Donn and down by the most northerly of the forest tracks – if you can find it. This continuation is for post-graduate sylva-navigators. There are other forest tracks not shown on the map; one which traverses at about 200 m links and/or crosses both ascent lines.

The eastern side of the mountain offers a snarl of cliffs and corries and the snows can linger long. At one time the local Mackenzie earl held his lands from the king on condition they could produce a snowball whenever it was demanded. Strathpeffer folks are inclined to make an ascent from the south but this involves crossing 16 km of uninspiring moorland. They also tend to make the ascent on an annual midnight walk.

A round of the eastern corries is a magnificent walk but the approach is a long one. There is a path of sorts up by the Allt nan Caorach, draining the corrie, which can be reached from Eileanach Lodge in Glen Glass, five miles up from Evanton on the A9 north of Dingwall. The road starts by the bridge over the River Glass in the centre of the village and is signposted 'Assynt'. A locked gate at the bridge leading to the lodge is as far as cars can go.

The most astonishing feature in Glen Glass is the Black Rock of Novar which is actually a mile-long, deep-cut gorge, which offers intimidating explorations. The walls are up to 150 ft high, often undercut, and lost in the jungle. The gorge has been leapt – once – and climbers have traversed it at water-level, both feats which are not likely to encourage emulation!

I've been up Wyvis eight times and the most common comment, on looking through my logbooks of those visits, is the bitter cold conditions met on more than half the ascents, whether in summer or winter. The most recent visit gave one of the coldest climbs I've ever had, anywhere, and unfortunately it coincided with the dog having a hormonal hiccup that led to the shedding of his winter coat in December rather than in the normal spring-summer period.

We'd met a friend off a London sleeper at Inverness on 4 January and headed for Wyvis, new to him, a good 'easy day' to start a holiday in the north. There wasn't much snow on the hill (it had all been blown off) and there wasn't much daylight either as the sky 'glowered', darkly streaked with rectilinear wind clouds. On the Glas Leathad ridge the cold was fearsome. In the time it took to take a photograph my fingers went numb and had to be painfully thawed out. The dog was miserable so I packed him in the rucksack but it was full of gear and, three times, he more or less fell out. Each time I put him back my hands froze. We reached the summit at a trot, carried along by this evil, hissing world of wind, so as soon as we turned, it took us in the face, battering the breath back down our throats. We baled off at once to lose height as quickly as possible but that was a slow enough process as the steep ground was frozen and slippery. Crampons wouldn't have been amiss on the steep, icy turf. Though well-clad and with windproof upper garments, head-cover, good mitts, etc., I'd not put on windproof trousers. Thick breeches and thermals should have been all right but I was suddenly aware of a burning sensation below the windproof level. The tip of my penis was freezing despite the two layers of clothing. It was only amusing in retrospect!

The first visit to Wyvis was not planned but my brother and I (and friends) had borrowed father's car and it ran into mechanical troubles at Durness. Limping south, my brother dropped the rest of us off to climb Ben Wyvis while he went on to Dingwall or Inverness in hope of repairs. We only set off from Garbat at 2 p.m. on a freezing, sharp October day that had me recording the view in detail in my log. I went on to collect all the Tops so, once the golden sunset had dimmed, I had fun descending through the hugging forest in the dark. It was too dark to see the map but all the drainage led to Garbat so there was no real worry. The frozen flanks of the hill were dangerously slippery that day as well.

The second ascent was a February one with spindrift swirling and bitter cold. Nearing the summit, I noticed a crack running along the crest: the cornice on the east side was ready to avalanche. In a misty day it would have been invisible ... We saw wild-cat prints in the snow and an eagle soared overhead. The weather was cold enough that a bottle of lemonade froze inside a rucksack. On the next four ascents I was by myself: one climb was made vile by steamy heat, one had to be hurried as a big storm was brewing in the west, one was a late April ascent from the east which again gave a wild, windy, snowy day (I'm now convinced Wyvis is prone to this windy/cold weather) and one was part of my Munros-in-a-one trip. Five years after that it was the first hill climbed after my return to Scotland at the end of my *Groats End Walk*, using a 'meeting-up day' of friends before our backpacking trip in to Seana Bhraigh. That was a chilly October day too, with the odd stag roaring and fieldfare blowing over cloudy ridges like autumn leaves. It was someone else's turn at Top-bagging. The rest of us ambled down, talking as only re-united hill friends can do.

The big snow of February 1978 – Newtonmore

Beginnings

The holds were there
somewhere
asking to be caressed
into a route of sorts.
Extremities
(finger tips and toes
not yet frostbitten)
were made aware
      – tinglings
          – tensions
              – tremblings

and laughter.
Rock rasped the core
of a pumping heart,
pulled in my slack
and belayed me
with cobweb delicacy
to the hard rock
of a daft game
I thought was reality.

The first frost found us out
Gaping at a lit moon.
Honed by the knife-edge of cold,
Salt-sharp, star-shivery,
We took refuge under the pines
And pulled on a pullover of past years
To face the winter ahead.
But the ice and the moon and the roaring
Zeroed our reality. Cold, moon, stags
Were all the present, our NOW –
Which is all the place
We can ever be.

STORM – THE STORY OF A DOG

The scenario was to become a familiar one. I'd met someone on the hill who would immediately say, 'You must be Hamish Brown.' Giving the ego a wee pat I'd humbly reply, 'Yes,' only to receive the regular put-down. 'Thought so. I recognised the dog.'

I'd never been owned by a dog before but Storm was special and I was quite content to be known as Storm's slave. I was just so lucky to have had those years with a very special companion.

I am not an animal sentimentalist, however much I like dogs. They tend to be like humans in that they come in all sizes, shapes and temperaments, likeable and unlikeable. Bad dogs are usually the result of bad owners and bad training, which is sad as well as bad. But in the complex, nasty world a dog can come to mean everything to lonely, elderly people, can be a joy to growing families, a companion for many at work and play. Their devotion to us is astonishing, and moving and so undeserved I often feel. Thinking of Storm's attachment I wrote:

> I have a dog who loves me,
> Loves me,
> And I love him.
>
> There's a difference in our love,
> Our love,
> He has no sin.

Sadly dogs' lives are shorter than ours and the fun and frolic is tempered with mortality. I've had one dog or another virtually all my life. Most were family pets, accepted as part of the scene, the pain of their departure softened by a new arrival. Storm was different. He chose me. He initiated a relationship which became very special and I loved him unreservedly in return, knowing even as I did so, that this would make the final parting a great sorrow. That was years ago now but it still hurts. Perhaps this is written as a catharsis, a palliative. I want to remember Storm in his prime, so very alive, in a high place with the sun haloing his bracken-coloured coat and the wind trembling his ruff with invisible fingers.

He lived a marvellous life and I'm unashamed at trying to recollect some of it in this self-indulgent story. Storm was a mountain dog so his setting was the hills of Scotland, England, Wales and Ireland: the Munros

111

and 'Furth' of Scotland. In his lifetime he covered all of these – an overall total of 459 Munros (and maybe 150 Corbetts). *Not* being with me on a Munro was unusual, and even if an article never mentioned his presence, photographs often indicated it. He was a very useful foreground and learnt to pose while I took colour *and* black-and-white photographs: two clicks of the shutter before moving.

When we were walking across Ireland as part of the *Groats End Walk* we came off the Galtymore Hills to re-provision at Mitchelstown. With shopping bags and a parcel of films, maps and Storm's *Frolic*, I sat on a bench in the square to sort out everything and repack the rucker. A tinker woman came along, leading a blind girl. When they drew level the woman asked, 'Can my girl feel your dog, please?' Storm played up as only Storm could, while the gentle hands ran over his soft coat. He gave her nose a lick. The girl looked blissfully happy and eventually straightened up, declaring, 'Sure, and he's a gorgeous fella.'

When our previous Sheltie, Kitchy, had died we didn't find a replacement right away but, after a couple of years, the dog-gap was being felt. A dog would be a good companion for mother, beginning to feel her years, and a dog is always a practical aid for home-security. We didn't do anything for two years and then a string of fortuitous events led us to Storm.

I was motoring home from three months in Morocco and had stopped off to visit Roslin Chapel, south of Edinburgh. As I drove up through the village I passed a lady leading two Shelties, two beautiful animals of sensible size. I pulled in and walked back to speak to her. Where did she obtain them? It proved fairly local so I drove straight to the address but there were no animals available or likely to be in the near future. They, in turn, gave me an address, in Fife, of people who bred Shelties.

Once the returning-home turmoil was over I rang this address but they didn't have any pups for sale either but did promise to get in touch when pups were next available. Many moons later I rang back as there had been no communication. There was an apology. The bitch had missed, so there were no pups. We chatted on and, with obvious doubts, she mentioned having an adult dog, a two-year-old, which they were wanting to part with. I wouldn't be interested in an adult dog would I?

Would I not!

One of the drawbacks of a new puppy was the man-hours I'd have to spend training it and seeing all its medical requirements were followed, demands beyond mother's failing powers and not at all convenient for me with my pressurised and erratic lifestyle. A grown-up dog might just be the answer. I asked if I could come along and see the dog.

At Coaltown of Balgonie I was shown into a living-room which seemed full of Shelties. Six were milling about and, as soon as I sat down, one came up and laid his head on my knees.

'Which is the one you want to sell?'

'Storm. The one who seems to have chosen you.'

Not long after I was driving home, Storm beside me on the passenger seat, sitting up, silent, and with that slight frown of his as he stared either ahead or, most of the time, looking intently at me. I must have passed the

Storm, 1987

test for Storm was utterly and completely my dog thereafter. As he was meant to be a family dog this could rankle with mother at times. Oh, Storm went with her all right but if I was there, mother would be ignored. Mother was a bit appalled when she opened the front door to find Storm sitting there, unexpected and unannounced.

Storm met his previous owner occasionally as she worked in the cash and carry I went to when stocking up for expeditions. She, naturally, would greet Storm with delight; Storm on the other hand, simply pretended she did not exist, which was rather embarrassing. Storm, for all his gentle ways, had a strong will of his own.

He had, and always did have, a strangely solemn look. People would want to pat him 'to cheer him up', because 'he looks so sad', whereas he was very happy, thank you, and rather disliked attention from outsiders. This even applied to other dogs. He liked meeting them, being with them even, but didn't join in romps on the sand. Maybe he'd had enough social life cooped-up in the kennels. Outwith the immediate circle of family and friends he largely ignored everyone. The 175-day *Groats End Walk* I suppose strengthened the initial bond between us.

That walk was described in a book and in it I wrote 'If by one of those twists of fate a lady in Roslin who had two Shelties ever reads this, then my blessings on you for being where you were when you were, and so

113

stirring me to action.' The book came out in 1981 with the paperback in 1983. In 1986 I received a letter from a Mrs Allan:

> I have been meaning to write to you for some time now . . . I made up my mind I am the person you met in Roslin with the Shelties. I am so pleased you have had so much pleasure and companionship from your dog Storm. I enjoyed reading about him. I am sorry to say I lost my two but like you I have got another, called Brownie (not small), a good companion, now coming up for four years . . .

Storm was a very proper, pedigreed sable/white Sheltie with a family tree going back to the g.g.g.g. parents, half of whom were champions, as was his sire, Fairona Rockafella. His mother's name was Philhope Precious Gold. For those into that sort of thing, the more important stables, I mean kennels, were Riverhill, Shelert and Flockfields. Storm's official name was Ellenyorn Spidersweb. Imagine yelling that from the back door at night. Some of his ancestry bore pretty weird names too: Ratafia, Swagman, Satin Slipper, Such a Lark, Golden Oriole, Rather Rich, Sweet Sultan, Strikin' Midnight.

This ancestry, apart from giving a slight giggle the two or three times I've actually looked at his certificate (usually when trying to find his medical record when his annual jag came up) means nothing to me. Dog-breeding strikes me as being a sordid manipulation of questionable validity. As far as Shetland collies go, in the last two decades, a breed of superb animals, of splendid temperament, always very fit and happy, have been turned into shrunken miniatures with neurotic temperaments, as far from the original working dog as real Shelties were from their wolf ancestry. What sort of sick humans can do this to dogs? Shelties were working dogs; now, as like as not, they are minute powder puffs, being led along city streets as a dainty accoutrement to their owners' mincing fancies. Thank God Storm was a bit on the big side. He escaped from the prison of show ring and stud yard. But it has taken just his lifetime to see the breed ruined.

Storm's pedigree had him described as being 'sable and white'; to me he was the colour of blowing winter bracken, his coat a mix of black, russets and white. His white ruff, like a lion's main, was so fluffy that, against strong light, it shone like a halo. This made photographing the dog difficult: he frequently had no outline! But his colours made him blend in to his country surroundings; so he could be hard to see.

Wildlife frequently didn't notice us and would wander up until, some-times, our fatal scents would startle. Hares were constantly doing this. In winter or spring they lope about with the abandon of children at play and I've seen us sit, the still hub of a showground whirl of crazy, circling hares. Storm, who is not a great one for playing, on one occasion so far forgot himself as to join in a wild hare frolic. The hares didn't seem to mind and at one moment he was chasing a hare and the next was being pursued himself. They were all daft on the golden spring snow that day.

When Storm climbed Ben Chonzie the snow had disappeared early so that hares, still in their winter white, stood out ridiculously – yet were convinced they were quite invisible. Poor Storm didn't know where to look. My rough count of hares visible was 54.

Coming back down the North Esk road one autumn there was a constant flurry of rabbits in the headlights. Storm, however dozy, would always come to life when we came to rabbit/hare/deer country, and sit with his nose glued to the air intake, high on an olfactory fix. He'd look up and watch awhile, sometimes running to the back to follow the flight of a roebuck or pheasant, but always returned to the obvious, rich pleasure of the air vent. When motoring, I'm sure this strong sense of smell gave him an indication of nearing destinations. Coming home, from any direction, he could be lying on the front seat, apparently asleep, but would suddenly sit up and look expectant as we neared Kinghorn. I could vary the approach line but he still knew. Movement could change but the landmarks were olfactory. When I took one particular road out of Kirkcaldy he would never lie down; he knew he was heading for my brother's. Turn off that frequented route and he'd give a sigh and curl up on the seat and bury his nose in his brush of tail.

On one visit to Nancy Smith's hostel at Loch Treig we went for a walk up the road. As we neared the keeper's house three terriers came rushing out and flew at Storm. There was chaos and in the end I lifted him and, while one terrier still yapped and jumped about, the other two dangled in suspension, with a good grip on Storm's thick mane. The keeper put his finger over their noses and they, perforce, let go. He decided the dogs, used for hunting foxes, had caught sight of Storm and assumed *he* was a fox! He did look like one and one reason I never let him roam was the danger of a trigger-happy keeper.

One of the funniest incidents on the hill began with us disturbing a fox. We were chuntering down a peaty slope west of Mount Keen and I jumped off the decayed bump of an old hag. Even as I was in the air I saw, through my legs, that there was a fox curled up in the lee of the black cornice. Its reflexes were remarkable. Before my feet hit the ground it was streaking across the slope. Charging through between two hags, it almost ran into an ambling hare which, in turn, went dashing off. The hare soon ran into a brace of grouse who let out a great complaint and went whirring off – straight through a herd of hinds. The deer didn't stay to ask what the panic was about and a hundred deer were soon mincing across the dark slopes. We were left standing, open mouthed, at this scene of relayed panic.

In those same hags on another occasion we once watched two daft hares go racing round a hummock. There was a moment of stillness then a distinct thump and two hares, limbs flying, shot up into view over the hag. They had run straight into each other.

Hares seem to be accident prone. On another occasion Storm and I were sitting in a reef of granite boulders, the only landmark in a sea of heather moor, when a hare came trolloping along, hare and us in full view, each of the other. The dog tensed with excitement as the beast came nearer and nearer and finally ran (still at full tilt) straight into the dog. With mutual looks of astonishment the hare disentangled and shot off only to take another header over my outstretched legs. It then set off again, looking back (with pardonable anthropomorphism I'd say it was mouthing curses at us) – and promptly ran straight into another big boulder.

I was reduced to hysterics by this triple slapstick act and, with hind thought, can only think the hare knew its environment so well that it was heading round that first boulder, where we sat, with absolutely no thought about its route. As a youngster I once had a squirrel do exactly the same, taking a header over my legs, because I was sitting across its regular run. More recently, in the High Atlas an elephant shrew made several sorties towards me and back under a rock before running over my lap and under the boulder beyond. I was obviously sitting on its regular route. So I suspect the hare just didn't see us. Part of the humour I'm sure was that this was just the sort of thing likely to happen to an absent-minded human – like me!

Subdued, natural colouring allowed us many interesting encounters with wildlife. I've never worn gaudy clothing and detest it in others for this very reason. Today's rainbow patterns must be a guarantee that the wearers see little. All wild creatures have sharp eyes. Camouflaged, you might get off with careful movement and see things; in the hyped-up, lurid, fashion-conscious gear of today, bird and beast will have miles of warning. This should be fairly obvious and I find it rather sad that it isn't. The truth is that many – most – walkers crash through the great outdoors with very little interest in the wilds and wildlife. They are there to indulge their egos and their gaudy garb is simply the outward show of their insensitive arrogance. 'We are the greatest' is the message, 'We are masters. See us. We don't care.' God knows how often Storm has looked up, speculatively, nose twitching and I've followed his pointing only to see, sometimes miles away, a procession of people, obtrusive as belisha beacons. The gain, just occasionally, has been their driving deer or other animals downwind ahead of their thoughtless march so these have run on to us, giving marvellous close encounters with wildlife.

By sitting still so much can be seen. One of my favourite birds is the long-tailed tit. These busy travellers (like flying teaspoons) working along riverside birch trees have often passed mere feet away from Storm and I lying in the heather. They are not easily deflected from their perpetual pursuit of food but if we'd stood up or been on the move they would have dashed off at once. A noisy family party of wrens were once working down such a burnside and one of the birds actually popped out of the heather and perched on Storm's head – to their mutual surprise. A lizard once ran over the dog's back and the sensation must have been like a tickle to a three-year-old because Storm, for the next half hour, was constantly quivering and giving his coat a shake.

Storm's first hill days were in the Ochils then, immediately after, we had a long weekend of Corbetts, not Munros, which was just chance, being a long-planned trip (Sandy, who I was with, has now completed his Munros, the fourth in our local club to do so) but using two cars and working through a landscape is something I'd recommend to all Munroists. For heaven's sake get away from the perpetual car-dominated, easiest-route Munro-bagging!

Green is the colour of spring: Storm by Loch Lochy in the Great Glen

We met up at Glen Coe on a Friday night, crossed the Corran Ferry early on the Saturday and went to leave my camper van at the foot of Glen Scaddle before heading for Strontian and the 1-in-4 road over the hills to then walk up Glen Hurich to Resourie Bothy where we worked on the surrounds for the rest of the day. Storm had lessons is obeying the order to 'Stay!'. He enjoyed his first bothy night. The next day we seemed to go up and down several glens, bagging wild Sgurr Dhomhnuill and descending to Glen Scaddle to be eaten by clegs at Tighnacomaire. We then walked out to my van, with several stops to plunge into golden pools. Storm did not like swimming. He was exhausted after encounters with herds of deer and free-ranging cattle. After a night in the camper the plan was to traverse Resipol back to Sandy's car, completing a lot of new ground, new summits and no repetitions of route.

A couple of weeks later we did the same sort of thing – bagging Munros this time – but using a combination of camper van and push-bike to make a decent sortie rather than car-dictated minimalist days. We'd been washed off Beinn Sgulaird (Storm not minding rain in the least) before driving north then west as the forecast suggested this might find better weather. The bike was hidden near the west end of Loch Cluanie and we descended Glen Shiel to camp at Dorusduain. It rained overnight but we went anyway: off from the Bealach na Sroine. At the top of the wood there was a notice saying 'Horses Please Shut Gate' to which a wag had added 'Humans Also Please Shut Gate!' We had a midge-free breakfast at the pass (still only 7 a.m.) before going off for A' Ghlas-bheinn, a complex little Munro whose gorges and lochans I've gradually explored over the years. Back at the rucker I brewed again, sharing the tea with a lad heading for Gerry's hostel, then dropped round and down into Gleann Gaorsaic. Everything was very dry so crossing the end of the loch was no problem. I checked on an old Braehead camp site out of interest but there was no litter, nothing to show we'd been there before. We met two others coming through the Gates of Affric, the Bealach an Sgairne, before we broke off straight up Bheinn Fhada (Attow) by a direct ridge. On both Munros we ran into hundreds of deer. Storm was off after them but a single yell was enough to bring him back. Deer, like sheep, were not to be chased. Over the years Storm, by *not* chasing away after wildlife, showed me hundreds of interesting things which his better senses picked up while I remained ignorant of their presence.

The weather was going so we descended by the corrie path and back down to Tolkien-sounding Gleann Gniomhaidh. Then it was round into the Fionngleann and the shelter of Camban bothy, a popular place judging by the bothy book. A Dutch lady blessed it as a haven from 'irritating tiny flies'. One guess as to their identity. Another suggested, after all the entries about rain, the bothy be renamed S.S. *Camban*. For most of the night the rain hammered noisily on the roof.

A look outside at six o'clock showed some improvement so we set off quickly, in hope. The Mullach is a big brute and I took plenty opportunities of photographing Ciste Dhubh and Ceathreamhnan and then botanised up one of the two Coire Odhar burns. Lush blaeberries were being enjoyed by beetles. The ascent ended as a race against 'rain from the west', which swept in remarkably quickly and caught us on the summit. The wind was icy and we raced off for the pinnacles and on up to A'Chralaig's huge cairn. We backtracked to the Top, which I feel should belong to it rather than the Mullach then, the sun out, returned to the Mullach and did the pinnacles again for improbable pictures of Storm. From the lowest point we ran scree down to a soppy corrie and then angled down over several burns. Storm suddenly dived over one to go straight to where I'd hidden the rucker, another trait that was to be useful in the years to come. (Once, coming off Macdhui I spent two hours searching for a rucksack I'd hidden a few hours earlier. Storm would have gone straight to it.) A brew set me up for the walk out to the main road and the bike hidden in the trees by Loch Cluanie. Of course the wind was strong from the west and the real watershed/descent lies miles west of the inn. And thereby hangs a Braehead tale.

We had been climbing peaks on the Cluanie Ridge and, some kids being more determined Munro-baggers than others, several opted to go down while the rest did 'just one more, sir'. We could see the weather was clouding so gave careful instructions to one group to wait right on the watershed at a certain time. When our second group kept the rendezvous there was no sign of the others. The mist was down. I grew worried. Then faintly on the breeze I heard voices and investigated to find the culprits cringing in the lee of a tin hut by a burn and cursing *us* for our failure. Weren't they at the watershed?

Once I'd cycled over the watershed my hands froze on the handlebars as the rain teemed down. I could hardly see. A caravan nearly knocked us over as it barged past and then *we* nearly caused an accident. Storm was in the rucker on my back and his grinning head out and perched high over my own, a spectacle that received odd and sometimes amused looks from the motorists coming up the glen. A big tourist bus passed and I was aware, out of the corner of my eye, of a whole passing array of startled faces as they saw the dog, but not me, whizz past just outside the window. When I glanced back it was to see the bus halfway up the roadside bank – the driver too obviously had his eyes on Storm instead of the A87.

One of Storm's first outings on to winter Munros was an ascent to the east end of the Cluanie ridge, using the old road over to Tomdoun to gain height and reach decent snow. The snow going up tended to be breakable crust and was diabolical on the descent. Storm, being so light, seldom broke through and, from the start, seemed to have sixth sense as to where to walk, a sense I was to trust on many a corniced ridge in bad visibility.

Back at the van we quickly threw our gear aboard and drove off for lower levels and kindlier climes. After a bit I made some comment about the dog, turning to give Storm a look. He wasn't there! I'd been so long without a dog that I'd driven off and left him behind. We drove back up the hill and met Storm trotting down the road with a rather resigned look on his face. 'What silly game is this new master up to now? Haven't I had enough schooling for today?'

Years later he had a post-graduate visit to the Cluanie Ridge. I went up on skis and we left the road to aim up on to the ridge between Creag a'Mhaim and Druim Shionnach. The corrie headwall looked steeper than anything I'd climbed on skis in the past but I put on *harsheisen* (ski blades that act as crampons) as well as the *skins* (artificial sealskin strips on the soles which prevent the skis running back downhill as one ascends) and carried on with more optimism than sense. There might have been a good, safe run-out below if I came off but it was a long way down and I could envisage losing a certain amount of epidermis from any slide. Storm was also finding the going difficult as the snow was too hard for his crampon-like claws to grip and I had to bash holes in the hard snow with my ski poles to give him something to grip. Eventually I found myself under a vertical wall, topped by a sneer of cornice. Stuck.

Well, nearly stuck, for by poking I found the wall was made of much softer snow so I might be able to fight up – but Storm wouldn't be able to. Pointing back down our track, I told him 'Go round!', which, rather reluctantly, he did, first inching down, splay-footed, from indentation to indentation until the angle eased and then half sliding, half romping the rest. I waved westwards. 'Go round!' He trotted on and chose an easy route up to rim the corrie on to the ridge.

Side-stepping up a vertical wall of snow was a novel experience and not exactly graceful but by battering with the skis and ramming the poles in horizontally I made exhausting progress. The cornice soon fell about my head, half of it going down my neck to melt instantly, the rest burying my skis and trickling off down the slope. Eventually I could reach over on to the top surface, stuck the poles in vertically and, pulling them at surface level, managed to do a sort of roll over and up on to the ridge. I just prayed there would be nobody up there to witness the odd sight of someone arriving, skis first, on to the crest. There was nobody but Storm who came padding along and gave me a lick on the nose while I was still in a canine position.

The ridge has a short, narrow section which, luckily, was not corniced but ran along in a wavering crest of snow, very pure and graceful so I felt a bit guilty at marking it. Halfway along I noticed Storm was not with me and in panic turned round. He wasn't far back, head and shoulders buried in the snow, tail waving slowly back and forth like a banner. Goodness knows what creature he was investigating. I turned round to continue but it was a much more thoughtful turn for, halfway through it, I realised that only the area below my feet had any contact with snow, the tips and rear portions of my skis were sticking out over space. It was a narrow section all right. Storm, of course, trotted along the crest as though it was pavement wide. He is very hard to live up to.

Dogs seem to be much safer than we humans and when they do take wallops they don't seem to break the way we do. When at school in Dollar, our family dog was a tough fox terrier which went with me everywhere, on the Ochils or in the Devon valley. One day I was walking up to the Castle with my girlfriend and her robust springer spaniel and, for reasons I can't now recall, Hamid got bumped off the path by the heavier dog. He bounced about twice on the way down the 80-ft drop and, luckily, landed in a pool rather than on the rocks. He crawled out a bit winded and then found a devious route back up the verdant cliff, apparently none the worse for his adventure. The humans were considerably shaken.

Storm seldom harmed wildlife; 'look but don't touch' had been drummed into him from the start. Sheep were taboo. I took him down to the Borders to introduce him to sheep right at the start. It was an embarrassing introduction.

The Meggat dam was being built at the time and in hope of some photos in early light I stayed above it in my camper. First thing in the morning, Storm and I jumped out to relieve our bladders. After he'd anointed a clump of rushes and had a good shake and stretch he looked up to see several sheep strolling past. Not having seen sheep before, he walked up, nose a-quiver, to investigate (he was well endowed with 'insatiable curiosity') and the wily ewes stopped, then walked on at an increased pace, so Storm had to hurry a bit, so the sheep started to hurry too. As I was pulling up my zip there was the classic scene of a dog apparently chasing sheep – and at that moment a Land Rover came round the corner. The shepherd!

Simultaneously I bellowed 'Storm' and the dog turned at once, to come back perfectly relaxed and unworried. Obviously obedient. I rather babbled out an explanation to the shepherd who, bless him, was quite understanding. 'I saw the dog obey instantly,' he said. 'I reckon you've a winner there. You wouldn't part with him?' Collapse of Hamish. Shepherds can judge dogs at a glance of course and Storm would have made a fantastic working dog. Only on one occasion did I ever have any unpleasantness with a shepherd because Storm was with me (described later) and often potentially angry situations were defused because the dog was so obviously well-trained.

I can remember once coming down to a glen where I had to walk along a farm track with sheep everywhere. As ever when we encountered sheep, Storm automatically came to and walked at heel. As he did so I saw a shepherd striding stiffly towards us. By the time we met I was leading a long procession of dog and about 50 sheep, all neatly in single file, nose to tail and the leading beast nose to tail with Storm. The shepherd's face was a study of conflicting emotions and as soon as I'd given our opening 'Aye' I'm afraid I just burst out laughing. So did he. We had a long chat about dogs and their training and the damnable people who take untrained pets into sheep country. My sympathies are entirely with the shepherds.

This lad told me of a recent experience where he had seen a couple with their dogs blatantly cross a field through a flock of his sheep. They had three dogs and these chased the sheep everywhere while the owners looked on quite unconcerned. The ewes were in the field for lambing so goodness knows what the damage was, quite apart from the ewes the dogs had worried. One ewe had to be put down.

Some time back a walker wrote to me following an unpleasant encounter with a farmer who had taken violent exception to his dog being on the hill. Had I, he asked, ever run into such hostility? My answer would be, 'Very, very occasionally,' and due, as much as anything else, to the variety of human behaviour. Much more often, as above, potential hostility has vanished on contact. I can only think of one occasion when it did not – at a farm which had the mixed blessing of the West Highland Way on its doorstep so I could sympathise if the farmer had more than his share of badly trained dogs to cope with.

He was busy ploughing in a field to the left as two of us and Storm walked past. Sheep to our right never moved at our passing. The dog never moved more than a few yards from my heels. The farm area was full of noisy poultry, goats and some stray sheep had to be passed to make our exit. Storm ignored everything. At this stage the farmer came roaring up on his tractor and opened with 'You can't take that effin' dog up here.' When I quietly explained I had every right, he immediately demanded that I put it on a lead.

My dog is controlled by quiet voice commands. If sheep are about he will come to heel without any command. He is a trained dog – which was patently obvious – but my explanations were simply swept aside under a torrent of invective. Enough was enough. I simply declared we were on a right-of-way, my dog was under control, legally and morally he had nothing to hold against me and we turned to walk up the glen. The encounter did nothing for the day's enjoyment.

The majority of hill walkers will have trained their dogs but, just as in all aspects of life, there is a silly and selfish minority who can cause problems out of all proportion to the overall situation. One wild dog can destroy a dozen sheep in half an hour. The shepherd who has suffered has every right to detest dogs thereafter. But there are shepherds who can be quite irrational even if they have not suffered. Compromise can often avoid confrontation. The lambing season and immediately before it is one time when walkers with dogs should largely avoid sheep country, just as in the stalking season a bit of compromise can avoid problems.

Vast alternative areas are available, spring or autumn – walkers can keep all the National Trust mountains for these seasons, for instance. There is also a certain call for plain common sense. Some areas *look* sheep-priority. Go round them rather than barge in. And read and listen and question. The more you know of the Highlands – from being in them – the less you are likely to find trouble. Sense and sensitivity is so very important.

There were many encounters over the years when I was asked if I'd sell Storm. The oddest was on top of Brandon, that magical mountain in the extreme south-west of Ireland. It has a long crest, cut away on one side into vast corrie with steep, cliff-beaten headwalls. Sheep were always going on to those slopes and falling down the cliffs I was told by the shepherd who I met staggering along under a load of stobs (fence posts). He was going to fence-off the cliff edge, an astonishing work for every post and coil of wire had to be carried up on his back from sea level to 3,000 ft.

While he was talking, Storm – the most placid and friendly of dogs – was receiving a bit too much attention from the shepherd's two collies. In the end he turned on them and, in seconds, routed both. Before I could open my mouth there was an awed, 'Do you see that now? You wouldn't be willing to part with your dog, would you?'

The one thing I never liked in Ireland was the habit of putting out poisoned bait for foxes or stray dogs. I kept meeting shepherds who had lost dogs through eating a dead rabbit, or whatever, which had been poisoned. Yet they were as apt to follow this habit as any. It seemed to be a blind spot but the Irish are not renowned for logicality. But it meant I could never relax a moment with Storm. He had to walk to heel most of the time in case, wandering ahead, he came on any tempting morsel – either to be eaten or rolled in. Why, incidentally, do dogs roll in the foulest of smelly corpses?

During one Hogmanay climb of Fionn Bheinn, that between-trains Munro above Achnasheen Station, we found a dog on the snow-blasted summit: a black-and-white collie, thin (even by working-dog standards) and too wary to be caught. It had obviously been there for some time, for the dog had melted a hollow in a drift where it had been sheltering till we almost stood on it. The beast stood in the blowing drift, head lowered, blinking along its nose at us but would neither come to heel nor allow us anywhere near. All we could do was leave most of our lunch for it to eat. We went in to inform Sid at the hotel so he could mention it to the locals and we phoned the police. We never heard anything more.

We once had a case of mistaken identity. I forget, now, on which Munro but, as Storm and I reached the cairn a gangly, bearded man stepped round the cairn. He glanced at me, then looked again, 'Are you Hamish Brown?' I half-smiled a 'Yes' only to hear a gruff 'I don't look like you at all' – and he strode off, with a sheltie following. It took a moment to guess the reason for his discomfort. Humph! His sheltie didn't look anything like Storm!

Later on there is an article I wrote about the Ben Nevis Observatory centenary celebrations. This makes no mention of Storm but he was there nevertheless – and ensured I missed the summit ceremonies. We lost each other.

Somewhere above the lochan, as the angle steepened, I began to work my way up through the long line of met. enthusiasts (who were not all fit walkers) and Storm, usually at heel, became detached among all the legs. When I turned to speak to him, he wasn't there! I let everyone overtake. No Storm. I hurried right up the line to the front. No Storm. I began to question people. He'd been seen running up and down obviously searching for me, then heading down the hill. I ran.

I ran because our start had been the distillery which lay beside the busy, dangerous A82. If Storm wandered on to it . . . When I arrived, gasping and legs quivering, there he was sitting beside the car. For a moment he looked rather embarrassed, even worried. How would I react? Had he done the right thing? My hug was instant reassurance, his joy ecstatic, my relief beyond expression. Full marks, too, for his behaviour. When he couldn't find me he simply went back to the start, no doubt back along a well-scented track across the moorland miles. Would humans in trouble have used as much gumption?

He became a very experienced hill dog in the end, not only in Scotland but on several trips to England, Wales and Ireland. Rhinogs, Brecon Beacons, Brandon, Donegal, High Street, The Cheviot – he knew them too. And islands – from Inchkeith at home to remotest Hebrides and Orkney and Shetland. He was with Colin and me when we were involved with the 1988

Boots Across Scotland attempt at doing all the Munros in a day. Our chosen peak was Beinn Bheoil, next to Ben Alder, and we canoed down Loch Ericht to base ourselves at Ben Alder cottage for a few days. Our days of canoe activity were 'brilliant', in Colin's parlance; the vital day, the first of May, was diabolical. We had a miserable ascent but some never made their summits. The 1992 attempt failed too. Roll on 1996.

The last canoe trip Storm and I made together had an ironic twist to it. We'd bag Munros along Loch Mullardoch by canoe! (Anything to avoid walking those shores.) As a youth, a sortie north had been stopped abruptly by finding the hydro had joined Loch Lungard and Loch Muller-doch. With my pre-war map I'd planned to walk between them. Launching was not easy. The tide was out and what looked like firm sand was just a surface skin on top of bottomless black peat mud. A slaistery start. Then halfway along, horror of horrors, the long drought had re-created two lochs and between lay the barrier of a rushing river!

Storm would steal food given half a chance. At a BFMC meet, camping at Strontian, I took a slide of him, rump in air, tail waving with pleasure. His head was invisible as it was through under the flysheet of a member's tent. Yelled at to 'come', he withdrew and trotted up, trailing a string of sausages behind him.

Ben the Burner (he worked at the local crematorium) told me a story about Storm at one of our Hogmanay meets at Suardalin bothy which the Braes o' Fife maintain. We had all gone for a day on Beinn Sgritheall, Dave and Co. leaving behind a dirty array of supper and breakfast dishes and pans. Storm and I arrived back first and, while I went off to fetch water, Storm set about licking all the dirty dishes. Ben, who had not been on the hill, said Storm made an excellent job of cleaning the pans and when Dave and the others returned they thanked *him* for washing all their stuff. Ben hadn't the heart to inform them of the truth.

Storm was not a water dog but he delighted in sea canoe trips, many being made from the sands below the house. If I was silly enough to paddle off without taking him on board he would simply swim after me and I was then faced with lifting aboard a very wet creature who would immediately give himself a good shake, which did nothing for the balance of the craft or my comfort. I soon learnt to make sure he was on board, in his normal fluffy and dry state, before launching.

John Muir had a similar problem with his partner's dog, Stickeen, during an Alaskan canoe trip: 'When we were ready to start he could never be found, and refused to come to our call . . . as soon as we were fairly off, he came trotting down the beach, and swam after us, knowing well we would take him in. When the contrary vagabond came alongside, he was lifted by the neck, held at arm's length to drip, and dropped aboard.' John Muir also commented on Stickeen's ability to read the signs ahead: 'He spent dull days in sluggish ease, motionless, and apparently as unobserving as a hibernating marmot . . . but . . . anything interesting, he would rest his chin on the edge of the canoe and look out. When he heard us talking about landing, he roused himself . . .'

Storm's chin rested on the sharp prow of the cockpit's coaming and in

The first Munro on the Groats End Walk, May 1979. Looking to Ben Klibreck from Ben Hope

the heat and shimmer he would blink and blink and eventually nod off, body sagging, so his neck bent and his muzzle would be pointing to the sky. Let a porpoise surface or a ship's wake rock us, and his eyes would open instantly for a quick perusal. Out at sea he always sat up when we approached land – but no way would he dive overboard as Stickeen would do.

He'd sit mesmerised when the Bass Rock gannets would power dive into the waters of the Forth or the Inchkeith puffins would rush past heading for home (a useful direction-finding aid if a *haar* came down). On one of those summer-drugged expeditions to Inchkeith we had made it back almost to Pettycur so I rested awhile before heading in to shore. This time I fell asleep as well and the tide had carried us to Dysart before I woke up again.

My canoe was an old wood and canvas kit model with a wide beam and open cockpit. It has taken me down most of Scotland's rivers and on many sea adventures, the best £5 worth of gear I've ever possessed. The gym teacher at Braehead had built it but, being short of cash, parted with it for the princely sum in the early 1960s. I'm still using it.

One reason I liked my old tub of a canoe was the assurance that, if I capsized, I could always climb in again. It might be full of water but would

125

still float and I could straddle the back and work forward into the cockpit a procedure which was practised every season, however unpleasant. Storm simply refused to go aboard for these inshore practice sessions but would sulk at the tideline, objecting even to the dying wash of waves wetting his feet. Heading to the shops, he would walk round puddles yet, in the wilds, bogs and burns were splashed through without any compunction. Fording the Luibeg Burn on one occasion, he showed uncanny judgment about river crossings – which completely convinced me that dogs can and do use intelligence and don't just do things by instinct.

The bridge upstream had gone so, perforce, I'd paddled across the powerful burn. The dog followed me out, from boulder to boulder, till he was left perched on the outermost granite block. I'd paddled across to a rocky spit opposite and Storm teetered on his boulder, eyeing the spit opposite, looking up and down stream, hesitating to plunge into the rush of water. You could almost hear the cogs turning in his brain. He eyed it all up once more then hopped back to the bank, ran upstream and out on to the boulders again, plunged in and made a perfectly angled ferry-glide across to arrive on my spit of rock. Had he plunged in from the initial spot, he would have been swept down past the landing spot. He knew this – and made allowances for the current. I found this astonishing.

He never liked having to swim rivers like that but, having eyed the options he'd soon splash in and cross. His hair would spread out on the surface but landing was made harder by this sodden pelt which must have weighed far more than the skinny dog underneath. People seeing the rat-like figure were always astonished to feel how very tough he really was. His muscles bulged like a weight lifter's. I never, ever, saw him exhausted, not in his prime anyway.

Now, a bothy tale. I'd just reached that pleasant limbo land between waking and sleeping when Storm sat up suddenly. I hoped it wasn't mice or I'd get no sleep at all. There is but one creature, and one alone, that Storm cannot tolerate: mice. I'm not so keen on them myself. Overhead they seem to wear hobnails, in the walls they sound like an avalanche, and inside a plastic bag of one's belongings they can create the most sleep-wrecking rustling. But it wasn't mice. Storm sat, tense, his face turned to the doorway, nose twitching, every line alert as I could see from the cold moonlight that managed to penetrate the cobwebs on the perspex window.

Eventually I picked up the sound of people approaching in the distance – and cursed. Snug inside my newly heated-up sleeping-bag, the last thing I wanted was a crowd banging in with their noise and bustle. I wanted my sleep. The sounds came nearer, then there was a silence, broken only by a faint sigh from the dog – who still sat gazing at the door expectantly. Yet Storm seemed tense rather than just his curious self waiting to eye up some potential soft touches for a biscuit or piece of cake. I noticed he was trembling. The party outside went on westwards past the bothy which, if welcome, was very strange. Even if they were camping most people will look into a bothy in passing. Unless they think it is haunted! After a spell the dog gave a long sigh, turned around a few times and lay down again in the crook of my knees, his usual spot.

I thought no more about the strangers who passed in the night, at least I thought no more about them until we were setting off at first light. I automatically looked along the glen to see if I could spot tents. The glen was empty. And then I felt distinctly uneasy. Our tracks in the snow were clear enough: our arrival tracks and the short excursion tracks leading to patches of yellow snow. But in that sweep of white in front of the bothy, across which both Storm and I had heard a party pass, there was not a single track in the snow. I have no explanation to offer.

Thinking of Storm and visitors reminds me of a camp we once had in Snowdonia. The dog (Kitchy in that case) was left at home for once. Ann, a fellow teacher and regular hill companion, was sharing a tent with me. In the middle of the night she suddenly sat bolt upright blurting out, 'But we haven't got Kitchy. We haven't got Kitchy.' I said I knew this and it was two o'clock. Please go back to sleep. She repeated the refrain and then said, 'I'm not having a nightmare. I just felt an animal walk over me and assumed it was the dog. Do have a look please.' I dug out my torch and there, curled up on some clothes, was a sleeping kitten.

Once, at a meet in Lagangarbh, a mouse started running round the skirting board. I grabbed the nearest weapon, which happened to be a cast-iron pan and set off in pursuit. Just at the moment Ann opened the door I managed to bring my weapon down on the mouse. At least it died quickly. I really hadn't realised the fragility of the mouse nor the forces involved in batting one with an iron saucepan. The mouse disintegrated and most of it was sprayed across Ann's legs. Like Queen Victoria, she was not amused.

I've twice had hedgehogs come into my tent. The noise they make can be considerable. A prickly flea-carrier is not the best companion in a tent, especially if one is sleeping on a li-lo. Storm seconded the orders for eviction. He likes finding hedgehogs. Always going up to the post last thing at night (when at home), I'm astonished how often we come on them roaming around the Kinghorn streets. I always collar the creatures and dump them in *our* garden to eat *our* slugs but they seem to be great wanderers. One day I noticed Storm standing at the west wall of the garden, sniffing so viciously his head jerked higher and higher till it was almost vertical. When I peered over the wall I didn't see anything at first then I saw the accumulated leaves at the foot of the wall were rising and falling steadily. Three young hedgehogs were hibernating in the leaves. I hope I didn't do them any psychological harm. Next spring they woke up on my side of the wall.

As like as not, my spring months were spent in Morocco and were then followed by May's Scottish coast-to-coast event and, as its originator and one of its organisers, I felt I had to take part if at all possible. This gave the heartbreak of leaving Storm again – just after we'd been reunited. Poor Storm; but we usually fitted in a few daft days in the wilds as I used my living in Scotland as an opportunity to ease the long walk by leaving supplies en route.

On any long trek one fights every ounce of the way so I used my knowledge of the Highlands to cross without camping or, if camping, I'd leave the tent beforehand where needed and then drop it off again once used. If ice axes were essential at the start and then no longer needed they'd be 'dumped' too and I don't know how often I left good antlers hidden for retrieving later on. Items like film, maps, as well as food or a change of socks, would be left with shepherds or keepers, at a B-and-B or post office, or, on some occasions, buried in some remote spot. These 'cache trips' as I called them became brief periods of liberty for Storm – and we had some good fun together.

I could not complain about the rule banning dogs from the Challenge; I made it. May is right in the middle of the Highland lambing season and not all dogs are as well-behaved as Storm! One bad incident and the event's reputation could have been ruined. In the first decade there was only a single case of people disregarding this ruling. 'Trail gossip' ensured their progress, with dog, was monitored across Scotland and when the man came in at the finish he was told he would not receive a certificate. He tried to excuse the dog, saying that it was really with his wife, who was not on the event but just walking with him. As he had been seen, walking the dog, on a lead, this excuse was given the pepper and salt it deserved. He had hardly chosen the most sympathetic of judges either as all three of us at the finish had just completed our crossings, all dutifully leaving dogs behind.

There may be some significance in our trio's dogs' names: Cloud (springer spaniel), Misty (alsatian) and Storm. The three dogs actually had a romp together on the sands of Montrose beach. Our simultaneous calling of this meteorological pack must have sounded odd to anyone within hearing!

Storm's predecessor, Kitchy, bore an unlikely name yet, on a remote Munro, we met a girl with a sheltie who was to call out 'Kitchy!' to her dog – and wonder why both responded. I've often wondered what the odds were of two dogs of the same breed, both called by a Malayan name, meeting on a remote hill in Scotland . . .

Ketchil San, to give him his full name (pronounced Kitchy) meant 'little one'. He'd really been father's dog, the friend and protector of an arthritic hobbler, enemy of postmen and all who dared intrude. He took his protective role very seriously. When father died he, willy nilly, had to go with me on school expeditions, the solitary guardian of an old man being thrown into the company of lively school gangs and for about a year he found this a somewhat traumatic experience before making the great adjustment and deciding these school kids were his responsibility.

We had a bothy in the Black Wood of Rannoch where many parties learnt the ropes of living in the wilds. In that crowded environment fluffy Kitchy was often stood on – and would react instantly with a bite. On one occasion he bit the wrong leg and an innocent bystander yelped; on another occasion there was a great clunk – he had bitten a table leg instead. The bites were never serious, being reflex reactions, and even as he reacted he would be stopping. There was no broken skin or blood or anything – just a very apologetic dog. After a year of this hurly burly he adopted the expedition kids, just the expedition kids, not all kids and fewer adults. In the playground boys or girls would come up with 'Oh, nice doggie' welcomes, only to be cut dead but, let a boy or girl appear who had been away at Rannoch or on expeditions, and he was all over them in tumultuous welcome. His world was divided into hillgoers and the rest, and the rest were ignored with a quiet contempt.

One shrimp of a lad adored Kitchy and made many trips with him. The youth emigrated and seven years later appeared on the doorstep, a hulking, long-haired, Australian. I didn't recognise him but Kitchy did. He was through my legs and leaping up in welcome, instantly.

Kitchy climbed all the Munros and his sum of Munros was well over 500 (Sgurr Alasdair was his last Munro *and* his 500th) besides many other hills, treks and expeditions by canoe or chasing after me on ski trips. He just lived for the hills but, like Storm, his last months were less energetic. Braehead School had closed down (due to the vanishing mining industry in Fife) and I took off on a sabbatical, climbing in countries round the world, with the dog, sadly, left behind. While in Morocco I received a vet's bill for 'putting down one dog and one cat' – and realised I'd probably never be seeing Kitchy again. When friends came out my first question was a direct 'Is Kitchy dead?' They had been briefed not to tell me (kind intentions) but they could hardly dodge my direct question. Yes, Kitchy was dead, as was Koko, the Siamese cat who had been Kitchy's great home friend throughout. Kitchy had been jumped on by a puppy while being walked by a neighbour. He suffered a stroke as a result. His back legs failed. The cat had been very ill a year before and had lost her Siamese cat's distinctive 'seal point' marking and was a rather startling creamy white, but seemingly in good health. Kitchy lay in a basket, unable to walk, and Koko climbed in beside him and the two just faded away together, the vet finally putting an end to their slow dying.

Kitchy's most exacting Munro was, naturally, the Inaccessible Pinnacle in the Skye Cuillin. There are plenty of two-legged hillgoers who have 'climbed all the Munros except the In. Pin.'. There is no walkers' or even scramblers' way up this blade of rock though, as a climb, it is not technically difficult. It is 'exposed', that mild climbing term for the feeling of a great deal of air below one as well as around and above. Luckily Kitchy was well-used to being in a rucksack when I scrambled or cycled so that was how he climbed the In. Pin. – on my back. Thank goodness he was a Shetland collie and not a St Bernard.

Each May Braehead had an expedition with English schools and on this occasion we were joined by Cheadle Hulme and Summerhill (Aberdeen) plus a former pupil, a student friend and even another dog: 17 could produce quite a circus atmosphere and the In. Pin. was draped with ropes as people climbed up and down. Fifteen and Kitchy made it to the top (not all at once!). Kitchy was so comfy in the rucksack he refused to come out – until he heard the rattle of chocolate paper. Most of the party set off for swims, tents and food but Jim, Kitchy and I sprawled for an hour on this lofty perch in heat-drugged ease before we thought of evacuating. Skye is like that.

We'd been aware that a couple of climbers had been fighting their way up one of the difficult routes on the vertical flanks of the Pinnacle. Eventually one seemed to be about to join us: a hand reached over the edge, piano-playing for a hold. Kitchy thought this curious and stepped over to have a look. ('For Pete's sake don't bite the bloke,' I prayed.) A grunt and a heave brought the climber level with the top where he found himself face to face with a dog. There was a look of utter disbelief and he lowered down again out of sight. I could just pick up part of the climbers' conversation which seemed to be somewhat argumentative: 'There is!' 'There isn't,' 'There is,' 'There isn't.' The leader popped up for another look and his voice echoed round Coire Lagan: 'There is so a – dog up there!' By this time I was lowering Kitchy off, abseiled off myself so, when the two climbers eventually landed on that tiny summit, there was nothing there at all. I'd love to have heard the conversation then.

It was almost 13 years later that Storm had his ascent of the In. Pin., an ascent in conditions that matched his name. I'd taken on the job of wardening the Glenbrittle Hut for the month of April and a memorable month it proved. I've just looked up my 'Summary' record book to see if conditions see-sawed quite as much as memory imagined. They did. I'll summarise the summary.

April 1	Clockwise circuit of hills west of Glen Brittle. Fantastic views of whiter-than-white Black Cuillin.
April 2	Storm up Banachdich, Ernst arrives.
April 3	Up the Coire Ghrundda slabs to frozen loch and traverse ridge to Eag: alpine action in a sea setting! (A picture of that day is on the cover of my anthology of twentieth-century British and Irish mountain poetry, *Speak to the Hills*.)
April 4	Portree and visit Collie's grave.
April 5	Mhadaidh from An Dorus, hard work as snow soft with thaw.
April 6	Ernst off so leave car at head of glen and lift to Sligachan. With Tim Winter and Storm (suitable names) have a great day on things between Am Basteir and Bruach na Freithe, desending the ridge to the Bealach a'Mhaim and out by Coire na Creise.
April 7	Complete exploring the hills west of Glen Brittle. Find a cup-marked stone.
April 8	Up the Sron and traverse round to da Bheinn to add Sgurr Mor for Storm. Back by the Sgumain snow shoot.
April 9	Writing and hut-tidying all day.
April 10	A soaker.
April 11	Local exercise, gardening.
April 12	Over Ghreadaidh and Mhadaidh.
April 13	Portree in wet.
April 14–16	Foul. Writing. Writing. Writing.
April 17	Day on Macleod's Tables. Sunny blinks. Black Cuillin stayed black.
April 18	Wettest yet.

April 19	Dearg (unintentionally) and, with army help, Storm up In. Pin., short side, icy, wet, manky.
April 20, 21	Rained off: the big thaw.
April 22	Gillean by Nicholson's Chimney – a snow climb! Add Am Bastier and Bruach na Freithe again.
April 23	Alasdair-Mhic Choinnich-Dearg (self, not dog, In. Pin.). Two days of perfection.
April 24	Have to go to Portree and shop. Still perfect.
April 25	Follow coast to Coruisk, up by the loch and bivvy up near the Glaic Mhor.
April 26	Home for breakfast. Hut busier. Evening out to bivvy at Rubh'an Dunain.
April 27	Explore Rubh'an Dunain – marvellous wildlife. Otters.
April 28	Traverse Maoile Lunndaidh – Sgurr na Chaorachain – Sgurr Choinnich (blistering hot) and sleep in van at Clava cairns.
April 29	Early pictures of the cairns and home to Fife.

Within those bare notes lies a great deal of contrasting fun and frustration. Our crazy weather can be guaranteed to exclude boredom from any Skye visit. The month began in superb winter conditions, then a spell of liquid assortments, and ended with a summer heatwave. Who needs to go the Alps or the Sahara?

Storm's day on the In. Pin, was memorable. We did not set off with it in mind but somehow I found myself heading up towards Sgurr Dearg and, having gone so far, well, we might as well at least make the summit of Sgurr Dearg. The night had been cold enough to glaze the sodden rocks and it was gruey cold, a dank, freezing, clinging cloud world which all sane folks would have carefully avoided. So I was surprised to hear voices and find young soldiers being heaved up and down the In. Pin., which reached out from the bowels of Sgurr Dearg like some obscene hernia, wiped by dripping cotton-wool clouds.

'Bloody idiots,' I thought and sat to watch the fun. A sergeant came and chatted and, of course, recognised the dog and asked about him. 'Had Storm done the In. Pin.?' Negative. 'Why not do it now?' Double negative.

So we did.

Under no circumstances would I have led the route in those conditions but with a top rope it would go and this would relieve me of having to find a partner and organise a climb later on. The climb was nasty for the rock was icy, even if much of the verglas had been bashed off by the feet of the terrified rookies – who were only too glad to sit and watch our performance. Storm was considerably bigger and heavier than Kitchy and my own weight-power ration had not improved over the dog years. I eased into the rucker straps and felt very out-of-balance just standing. Storm grinned out from over my shoulder. After climbing up the left side there's one more right-wards which I've never liked, being basically an old-fashioned balance climber, and with the extra weight I yelled a warning that I could peel. Maybe Storm noted the sharpness in my voice for he turned and gave my ear a lick. I couldn't fall off after that canine encouragement and scrabbled over and up efficiently enough, if hardly gracefully. My next dog's going to be a Yorkshire terrier.

If Kitchy gave us an amusing escapade on the In. Pin., Storm's contribution came on Sgurr Mhic Choinnich. We had scrambled up on to the lower end of Collie's Ledge, a rising traverse line across the huge Coire Lagan face of the peak. The ledge varied in size but the confident climber more or less just walks along it.

Mhic Coinnich has a long, sloping roof leading to its summit and then drops sheer beyond. This prow gives a good climb but not for me with the dog, even with a top rope – which was not available in any case. Collie's Ledge runs up across the wall to gain the rooftop in easy fashion, a very useful bypass. We set off along this.

Looking ahead, I noticed two girls coming the other way; obvious beginners, they were finding (as we all do) that exposure is something special in the Cuillin. They were not happy, even roped-up and treating it as a climb, moving one at a time with a face-to-the-rock shuffle along the perfectly adequate ledge. I paused at the corner, thinking it would be the best passing place but Storm went on in jaunty fashion quite oblivious of the 1,000 ft of nothing a few inches off the port side. The girls were far too gripped to see him coming and he went straight up to the leader and stuck his wet, cold nose right on that inch of skin that appears between breeches and stockings. A piercing scream rang out and I cringed into my corner with visions of the girl having leapt off the ledge. She hadn't but the thought of confronting them dismayed me enough that I wiggled right back in my corner and let them pass without seeing me. Storm came back and nosed me out and we completed the traverse and so up Mhic Coinnich. It was only later I began to chortle as I imagined what the girls' comments might be. There they were, roped-up, gripped on a fearsome traverse, when suddenly a dog comes along all by itself.

The most magical moment of that Skye trip came during our bivvy trip to Rubh'an Dunain, mentioned in one of the Skye pieces. We'd sat by a loch for breakfast when otters turned up, a mother and two greedy youngsters. They slowly worked towards me and landed on the rocks less than ten yards away. Both Storm and I froze, though I could see the dog's nose quivering as he tried to scent these unknown creatures. They splashed in and out a few times before the adult became aware of our presence. She stood upright to have a good look at us – and then came forwards slowly till she and Storm were nose to nose. Neither showed panic, neither showed aggression, to which I put down this extraordinary encounter. Having sniffed each other, the otter returned to the loch and Storm sprawled back on the ground. I breathed again.

The play wasn't over though. In a few minutes the otter was back, this time with a big, lively eel. The youngsters were all over her, begging for this tasty prey, but she had other ideas and swung the eel round away from their reach. A sandpiper had been sitting on a rock, bobbing up and down and wondering if she should move when, out of nowhere, she received a whack from the eel which sent her splashing into the loch. Her language as she flew off was unrepeatable. This bit of slapstick broke my discipline and I laughed outright. Exit otters.

Storm had one other amusing Skye episode, on Am Basteir. We'd worked along and down the wee wall so there was only the rooftop final ridge to go. This is very narrow and very exposed: steep on the left, sheer on the right. A twist of snow still lay along the crest and Storm, who seems immune to exposure, decided this snow would be excellent for rolling on. It may have been enjoyable but it was anything but good for my nerves. Storm rolling about, feet in the air, inches from a 300-ft overhang. He went on the lead. Of course, as soon as we proceeded, we met someone coming the other way – which made me feel the complete twit, with dog on lead for walkies. The reaction was immediate though.

'Hello! You must be Storm!'

This fan of Storm's, after brief conversation, asked if he could take a photo of the dog. 'Sure,' I replied and the great poser posed. The man looked up, then waved me to one side.

'Would you mind getting out of the way?'

My reply was, yes, I would mind. I hadn't brought my parachute or a 600-ft abseil line.

It was about this time I received a letter forwarded from a newspaper which I thought might have been a spoof from some of my friends (spelt minus the r) but eventually decided it was genuine as the hand indicated somebody elderly. Let me quote it in full.

7–8–78

Dear Sir

I was appalled to read in *The Sunday Post*, 6–8–78, about your Dog Storm who is to climb mountains with you.

Don't you think this is cruel. The poor animal could be frightened out of his wits and terrified at the heights he has to climb. Please don't be hard on him, he looks such a beautiful Dog.

Yours sincerely
one who cares for Animals

Reverting to Kitchy; a rather sad episode occurred in the middle of my sabbatical after Braehead closed. Home from the Andes and preparing for wandering the length of Africa, I had one day of happy liberty in the Lake District, a fine ski traverse of Helvellyn.

Kitchy too had always found skiing a frustration. Heading down, I could go faster than he could and he would be left running along my track or floundering through looser snow with his sharp feet, with the additional annoyance that I never kept on in a straight line but would swoop one way and another – very frustrating. Eventually he learnt just to sit and watch for several minutes till he could gauge my general direction. He would then head down the fall line while I looped back and forth. No flies on Kitchy either.

I approached Helvellyn from the north and after a couple of hours of skinning along came to the last slope leading up to the crowded summit level. Coming up from the right (west side) was an obvious school party of about ten. Kitchy spotted them at once and let out a yelp of glee and set off to greet his long-absent companions. As he closed with them he barked a welcome but suddenly he stopped and 'drooped', then turned back towards me looking utterly miserable. Whether he scented them or it was just the non-Fife accents saying 'Hello doggie' I don't know but he'd suddenly realised they were not his people. Poor Kitchy. That part of his life was over though he knew it not. So much for being cruel to my dogs. They lived on and for the hills.

Naturally, Kitchy having done so, I wanted to see Storm round all the Munros and this took five or six years to accomplish. It led me to a ridiculous seventh round in the passing and at times our interests conflicted. Before completing the Scottish 3,000ders, Storm had already been over the English, Welsh and Irish 'threes' linking them in a six-month continuous walk from John o' Groats to Land's End, the story told in *Hamish's Groats End Walk*. He has visited Ireland on several occasions but his first hours on Irish soil were pantomime.

He had been caged on the ferry across from Holyhead (we had no vehicle) and when we landed I asked directions for a cousin's house and we were cheerfully sent off in the wrong direction. An hour later we sat wearily with a curry carry-out on the church wall in Dun Loaghaire (where we'd started) when the church doors opened and hundreds of people streamed out. Across the water this might have been an embarrassing situation but not in Ireland.

A dozen men were soon arguing as to how I should reach my destination. One man produced the comment 'Jasus, you can't get there from here.' When we did reach the house it was empty. Kind neighbours took us in for tea until the key came (my cousin had gone off to Galway) and in the middle of nibbling barn brack I noticed a flea on Storm's coat. I grabbed this and for the next hour sat with a clenched fist . . .

Near the start of that long hike I'd been involved in a radio programme with Alistair Hetherington and Gordon Adam and was 'interviewed' in the hotel at Scourie. Storm was tied to a stool out of the way and the recording commenced. Storm spotted his food dish and went for it, only to find he was leashed. He tugged, the stool squealed across the linoleum and a paw sent the tin dish clattering. 'Who needs a sounds-effects department? Let's start again.'

He has starred in several bits of filming for TV and in Bristol a good scene was set up and rehearsed in a park above the Avon. Storm was to appear and, at a call, run across and leap up into my arms. He did this several times perfectly then, when the cameras were rolling, his dash stopped abruptly at an intervening tree and he stood against it on three legs. I'd swear he was grinning!

His leaping into my arms at a bidding had its more practical side on difficult terrain such as the Cuillin Ridge but even there, frequently, when I thought he would need assistance, he would appear *above* the problem part, having found his own way round.

One Hogmanay we stopped off at Nancy Smith's private hostel at Fersit by Loch Treig to organise Storm's last Munros. I seem to have known Nancy all my life. A lovely person. We'd been together in the Atlas and she hoped to go again, if spared. She was not spared and on a bleak, sleety day she was laid to rest at Kilmonivaig, as beautiful a corner as you will find but now tearfully hallowed by the crowd who came to say farewell. So many happy memories. But that was years on from Storm's last visit. Storm wanted the four Munros on the other side of the Bealach Dubh from Ben Alder. I went along as his chef and porter.

Beinn a' Chlachair (which sounds like the name of a single malt) was climbed on the way in and before reaching Culra Bothy we left the rucksack to add Carn Dearg as well, which is very much an eastern tail peak to the main body of Storm's ridge of peaks. That left three, which we planned to traverse to exit from their western end. The bothy was dank from heavy use over Hogmanay and a gang of Fife lads and I preferred to stand and blether outside under a crisp, starry sky. Storm, inside, gave their frying pan a good clean (not the first time he'd performed such a service).

In the morning it was snowing and we tramped the miles up to the Bealach Dubh with all the icy patches disguised by the new powdering. We both had some exciting slides. The pass was bleak, with the mist down and the wind moaning in the sad wreckage of a crashed aeroplane. Geal Charn, our first hill, culminates in a featureless plateau and to ensure we actually found the summit cairn we first wandered up to the summit of Lancet Edge, so we could take an accurate bearing over the wasteland miles.

We had two miles to go over complex country yet the cairn loomed out of the gloom as and where expected. It had to – 50 yards on there was a sneering edge of cornice. Two swooping drops and ascents on the grand highway of ridge took us over Aonach Beag (there isn't an Aonach Mor) to Beinn Eibhinn *the beautiful hill*, an appropriate place for Storm's 277-up. He promptly anointed it!

Storm had come a long way from his restrictive years as a show dog. It appals me that so-called dog-lovers can go in for genetic engineering and the sort of slavery the show ring entails. After the *Groats End Walk* book came out I showed Storm's previous owner the book. On the cover Storm sits with Snowdon behind him, and she turned to her boss (owner of Storm's brother), showing him this and saying, 'Isn't he grand? You'd never think he's had a broken leg as a puppy,' which was the first I'd heard about that.

Though I didn't know it at the time, Storm's last Munro (his 459th) came one Hogmanay when we were based in Torridon. Shortly after, I was off for months in Morocco as were others at our house-party. All these things came together in an article I did for *Climber and Hillwalker*, which was used in the next year's Hogmanay number. By then Storm had gone. Here is the article, for Sgurr Ruadh is a splendid Munro in an area which would be much more highly regarded had it been set anywhere else but facing the Torridon Triptych of Eighe-Liathach-Alligin.

Camping below the Triple Buttress of Coire Mhic Fhearchair, Beinn Eighe

Storm's Last Munro

Sitting by the cairn we looked across to the battlements and turrets of Liathach, Alligin, Beinn Dearg and Beinn Eighe, 'arrayed like *Ksour* down the valley of the Draa to Zagora', I joked. A month later I was there, among the battlements and turrets of desert castles, looking north to the long, snowy crests of the Atlas Mountains, strangely reminiscent of Hogmanay back home. There's a schizophrenic aspect to wandering among mountains.

Our view to the Torridon kasbahs was from Sgurr Ruadh – the highest of the Munros and Corbetts which crowd the country between Torridon and Glen Carron. We had not even set out to climb it. For our first Hogmanay outing we merely wanted to wander up Fuar Tholl, a choice made to suit the dog. He had done all the Munros and Corbetts locally except Fuar Tholl, so for his sake we drove round to Achnashellach and headed up the familiar path to Coire Lair.

The Railway Cottage garden looked trim and tidy, even in midwinter. Peter Hainsworth, a retired gardener, has carved a sanctuary out of the spreading *Rhododendron ponticum* and filled it with choice alpines and a fern house. (On odd days in early summer it is open for the charitable *Gardens of Scotland* scheme.)

Achnashellach Lodge on the other side of the railway track, an excellent walking base for those wanting greater luxury than Gerry's hostel just up the road, also has a superb garden setting with paths wandering down to Loch Dughaill through some of the tallest trees in Scotland and dozens of different rhododendrons. We've rounded off a few good hill days with equally good dinners at Achnashellach.

Wandering through Achnashellach station I retold the tale of the unfortunate lad I'd come to meet off a train one Hogmanay. He, burdened with rucksack, had cheerfully stepped out of his carriage, assuming the platform was as long as the train. It isn't, and we eventually found him down among the rhoddies, arms and legs waving like an upside-down tortoise.

We followed the path up by the river through the Scots pines. The boggy start was frozen into clean hardness and the puddles all had lids of opaque, glass-like ice which smashed noisily underfoot – a noise that fully satisfies the schoolboy heart of winter walkers. As the trees thinned out we caught up with another two lads and talked and walked together or drifted apart as chance decided. They were staying in the cottage next to ours and we found friends in common and hill memories to share.

An end-of-the-year sun lit the landscape and height was gained very easily. We turned off the Coire Lair path on to the one that wends up to the col between Fuar Tholl and Sgurr Ruadh. The muted Allt Coire Lair presented few problems and on the glacier-scoured slabs above we stopped to let the sweat dry off our backs.

The rocks were deeply scraped with parallel lines, the striations of a not-too-distant ice age. The vanishing glaciers had also left behind scores of sandstone blocks which were scattered in 'promiscuous abundance', to misquote Dr Johnson. Coire Lair is a magnificent natural museum of glaciology. As we continued up the path the Mainreachain Buttress appeared, a great thrust of verticality, black rock in a white world of snow. The record of climbs on its faces reads like a *Who's Who* of mountaineering.

Our path was a ribbon of ice and we walked more beside it than on it. After humming and hawing as to what to do we simply followed the path to the saddle between the peaks, which kept our options open. An Ruadh Stac and Maol Cheann-dearg suddenly loomed across the Coulags Glen, impressive in winter glow.

We had some food and watched two other walkers picking a route through the jumble of rock bumps, piled moraines and jigsaw lochans as they headed for Sgurr Ruadh. We followed of course, greedily accepting the two peaks available for the sweat of one.

Years before, I'd been staying at Gerry's hostel and had made a traverse of Fuar Tholl to this col in cloud. At the col a compass course became advisable and it was then I discovered my compass had disappeared through a hole in my cagoule pocket. (I found it later in the hostel garden where I'd donned my cagoule.) I don't know how many times I tried to make a way through that maze of bumps and lochans but twice at least I simply walked right round bumps on to my own track, still convinced I was more or less heading on a straight line. In the end I won through and the steep slopes beyond had to lead to the summit of Sgurr Ruadh. Descending was easy, backtracking, except for the spaghetti variations on the col.

Our cold, clear but hazy day presented no such problems and we wandered across the face above the Coulags Glen to follow a rake to its end, then scrambled up scraggy steeps to the final boulder slopes. Clach na Fionn in the glen below is a big erratic – one of many such which became linked with the early Fianna legends. Bran, the great hunting dog, was tethered to this rock, the Stone of the Fingalians.

So we arrived at the circlet of stone that crowns Sgurr Ruadh. The other two arrived a bit later and then two more, at great speed, the sweat streaming down their faces. Charles and I, sitting with cups of coffee and Christmas cake, felt not at all put out by such a show of zeal. Storm, the dog, found them a negative source of food. He is past master at sitting before piece-eating groups with a look that pleads, 'Please feed me, I'm really desperately hungry.' His success rate is about 99 per cent. He got a mince pie off Charles.

We chuntered down again, keeping to the deeper snowy areas to avoid the bare screes, or twisting between little crags draped with ice. Storm shot off one crag, having hit an ice boss on its edge, the sort of mistake he would never have made in younger days but now his eyesight was poor and his heart failing, though we knew it not. He fell about ten feet and walloped on to his side, stood up, and carried on as if nothing had happened. If either of us had made that sort of aerial display we would have ended as a casualty statistic.

The other walkers were not far behind us as we began the toil up Fuar Tholl. The first bump had some craggy bits to play on and then we were passing over the nape of the Mainreachan. We slowed, hoping to catch those following figures to give scale to photographs but they failed to appear until we were ready to leave the summit cairn. We didn't see them again and they must have made most of the descent in the dark. We juddered down a series of snowy gullies to reach the lower slabs, which allowed clean, quick progress to the moorland skirt of the hill. At Achnashellach we met the first pair of the day again and two other groups, all back safe and sound, as the early dark drew a veil over the winter daylight.

Fuar Tholl is *the cold hole* and usually lives up to its name. This day it was the views from its blockhouse of a summit which held us in thrall. The colours were all pearly greys and pinks. The sun set without a flourish and the first stars had been thrown into the sky by the time we'd fought the rhoddies and crossed to Achnashellach station. It had some decent lights we noticed. Previously a time-switch system gave just ten minutes of light before the train was due and five minutes afterwards – except that trains never did arrive on time so the illuminations lit a solitary world of snow and passengers invariably disembarked in pitch darkness!

The railway line runs behind the lodge/hotel and the station was originally built to serve that place. Edward VII stopped off to stay there and, stalking, nearly came to a sticky end when part of the Mainreachain avalanched. Achnashellach also saw a ridiculous early accident when a mixed train became detached from the engine during the run down Glen Carron. At Achnashellach the driver discovered he wasn't pulling anything. So what did he do? He drove back up the line to look for his carriages!

We juggled about changing our sweaty socks and clothes beside Charles's frozen-up car and noticed others were doing likewise. Coire Lair had had quite a few visitors that day. We called in to have tea with Gerry at his hostel before driving back to base at Torridon.

That night Charles and I went over plans for climbing in the High Atlas a few weeks later. There's actually nothing schizophrenic in this at all. Our Scottish hills and all foreign hills are just part of a single game. There are no horizons which we cannot seek to cross. Achnashellach to Zagora is as natural as one year slipping into the next, looking to the battlements and turrets of Torridon need be no different than looking to those of Irghil M'Goun. Hills, like Hogmanays, have no boundaries.

While I was in Morocco, winter/spring 1990, Storm had been unwell, something he'd eaten perhaps, but he was lively enough for my brief spell at home and had several good walks along the sands from Pettycur Bay. Valerie and Ian had lost both their cats while I was away and identikit black and white kittens, Jack and Jill, had taken their places so it was quite good that Storm was there to be accepted by these superactive mites. In no time at all I seemed to be saying goodbye to Storm again and was off for most of May in Morocco.

My homecoming thereafter was not so cheerful; the meal on the London-Edinburgh flight gave me a good dose of the runs and it took a week of pills before I recovered. (As I'd spent months in Morocco free of all tummy troubles the irony of the situation was noted though hardly appreciated.) Valerie and Ian dropped Storm home and he was not 100 per cent either as he was periodically lurching about, a stagger which had come on just a couple of days before and which could be a worsening of his old leg trouble. It was twisting much more noticeably when he walked.

I had to drive to Montrose the next day and when back I was much more worried about Storm's unsteady state than my own. That evening he made a bit of a hash of walking down the steps into the seaside garden. (I carried him up and down after that.) Not long afterwards I heard what sounded like the cries of a gull coming from the garden. Gulls often called overhead or out to sea but this was below the sun-porch level. I went over to look out into the garden, and there was a very distraught Storm in the big pond, desperately trying to scramble out, and yelling his head off — what I'd taken for a gull crying. He'd obviously lost his balance and fallen in. Next day I took myself to the doctor and Storm to the vet. Pills for both of us.

The vet thought that Storm perhaps had an infection in his inner ear which would account for his balance being upset and possibly there had been a mild stroke. At his age he'd maybe not really recover. So he had a course of antibiotics — and recovered splendidly! The next day was miserable for both of us. My new Transit van had been booked in to Auchterarder to have windows inserted, the first big step in converting it into a caravanette. We took it in at 8 a.m. and were to collect it in the afternoon. The state of my bowels meant we both staggered from café to café, and I sat over token cups of tea and on a variety of thrones in small back rooms. Storm as like as not was allowed indoors, for it was a grey day of Ochils dampness. When we did go for a walk round the Provost's Walk Storm headed for the river for a drink and when he shook himself he tumbled in. I pulled him out and dried him with my vest. I then had an upset and had to find a drapers and buy fresh underpants. It was not a good day.

However, we were both over the worst and in the two months of high summer spent most of our time working in the field on the route of the *Pennines to Highlands Walk*. Peggy made her spring visit and much of it went with the three of us tramping sections of the Antonine Wall and visiting Falkirk, Kilsyth, Kirkintilloch and the Roman bathhouse at Bearsden. Keith Anderson and I then walked the section from Byrness to West Linton, in blazing June sunshine. (In sad September — also a heatwave — we did the rest, from West Linton to Milngavie — a Storm-haunted walk.) Our first day, over the Cheviots and Dere Street to Jedburgh was a marathon. That evening I drank about ten glasses of water, three cups of tea, three of coffee and a pint of lemonade. Storm, even stripped of his winter underlay, would have found that heat punishing so I'm glad we opted to leave him with Valerie and Ian.

As soon as I'd collected him again we went back over the route, with the van, following-up 'matters arising' from our trail trial. Storm delighted in that sort of trip as we were in and out of the car a score of times each day and every wee walk was an olfactory and physical joy.

Typical of the sort of thing we had to sort out was creating a temporary route onwards from Jedburgh to Melrose – a long day but with plenty of interest en route: the Woodland Centre, Peniel Heugh's Waterloo Monument, Dryburgh Abbey, Scott's View, Newstead. A footbridge over the Teviot was still years away perhaps and our alternative by Nisbet added too many miles. So we followed the ancient drove over fields down to the charming old Teviot Bridge, a much better route. The view having been too hazy when with Keith, we climbed up Peniel Heugh to take photographs from this remarkable Borders viewpoint. We then went to visit Dryburgh Abbey. There are no shortcuts in doing a field guide – and Storm came to know that route every bit as well as I did.

There were odd days at home and a weekend at Ingleside looking after Sam and Emma so Valerie and Ian could attend a function without their dogs. After that we had a night on the Lomonds and climbed East Lomond in the kindly golden light of a summer morning – escaping from the van where I'd been reading-up on Linlithgow which was on our *Pennines to Highlands* route. A couple followed us up and they recognised Storm. They were from Linlithgow!

A few days later we were standing high on the hills south of Linlithgow, visiting Cairnpapple, one of the most exciting prehistoric sites in Scotland. Storm was left at the custodian's hut while I climbed down into the tomb. When I came back for the usual tail-wagging welcome the custodian said, 'What a nice dog.' Perhaps ominously, I noted in my log that Storm seemed to be finding uphills hard work. My mid-August 'birthday hill' was Cockleroy, also above Linlithgow, which we reached by walking from the historic town up to Beecraigs Country Park, then Cockleroy itself and back down by another route – a good day's walk and giving us a superlative Lowland viewpoint. Bass Rock to Arran, Pentlands, the Forth Estuary, Ochils and Highland Hills, a quite remarkable sweep for a wee hill.

Heading up the final steep slope proved quite an effort for Storm. He took it very, very slowly, with rests and much panting. I'd never seen him less energetic. Warning bells rang. Had it been any further, I would have carried him but I also thought if he was going to have a heart attack and die Cockleroy would be as good a place as any for his last walk. I slowed down to his pace. I thought, too, that if we had spent this year in Corbett-indulgence he would probably not have completed them: his 90 to go was too much, many of these being remote and demanding ascents. The last year, of these little forays as we created the *Pennines to Highlands Walk*, had been perfect for his failing powers. A few minutes on the summit saw him fully recovered and he bounced his way down again, tail flag-waving as ever. Life in the old dog yet!

There was a view indicator as well as a trig point on top of Cockleroy so I was able to perch the camera on the former, set the timer and dash back to sit with Storm beside the trig. It was only one of a handful of pictures I'd ever taken of both of us together. I didn't realise then that it would be the last. A print of it now hangs in my study. Some day I'll be able to bear looking at it.

Storm's last night in the van was by the Union Canal. We saw the passengers from the *Pride of the Union* having a barbecue meal by the Almond Aqueduct and, once the barge-restaurant had chugged off back to Ratho, Storm went over the grass with the efficiency of a vacuum cleaner. Not a morsel of dropped food escaped his twitching nose. Next day I was shown over Niddry Castle, in the throes of restoration, and then we went to join Helen Robotham, one of the canal rangers for a walk at the spectacular Avon Aqueduct. Later I returned to take some pictures only, back in the car, found I'd left an exposed film at the aqueduct – so we made a third visit that day to this spectacular piece of canal engineering (Telford inspired). This time we walked down and paddled the Avon. Storm seemed quite glad to splash in the water for it was a day where walking left one wringing wet with sweat. I was kept busy writing-up all I'd learnt that day till past midnight and spent the next two days in the dark room, then had a busy day in Kirkcaldy. I noted in my diary that 'Storm was romping with the cat last thing at night. Fuji seemed to be calling every day these days.' Fuji was mother's Siamese; when she died it had gone to the people next door, who had Fuji's brother. I just couldn't look after a cat, not with my wandering lifestyle. Storm and Fuji were great friends. Eventually I had to put Fuji out and tell her to go home. As usual it was away past midnight before I went to bed. Dear God, what a night it was to be.

A brief note on the layout of the sleeping area of the house would be useful at this point. At the east end of the house, off the main hall, was a tiny vestibule with doors leading to my tiny bedroom, the bathroom, a linen cupboard, study and spare bedroom. My bedroom was my original study and still had a large desk shelf where I sometimes worked on overspill projects. At this time I had two books on the go at once and maps and papers had so spread over desktop and bed that I decided to sleep in the spare room for a week or two rather than have to clear my bed each night. Storm transferred to sleeping on the bedside rug in the spare room.

The vestibule had a night-storage heater in it which had set an interesting problem when I had refurnished the spare room not long before. I decided a single bed would make it much roomier but as the next three visitors staying were all couples I had to revert to a double bed – but a modern one, on slimmer lines than the original Victorian monstrosity. I bought a smaller wardrobe too and, after it was wiggled into the room, discovered the large one could not be removed as the heater had reduced the passage through the vestibule. In the end the wardrobe had to be demolished *in situ*, with a sledge hammer!

Storm had become much more of a sleeper in his old age. A single squeak of a bed would once have had him opening an eye in the expectation of my rising, but latterly I could get out of bed, step over him, dress and go off for breakfast while he slumbered on. It did cross my mind that one morning he would simply not wake at all. I rather hoped so. I'd hate Storm to suffer. Strange how we are willing to have our pets put down to save them misery and suffering yet we waste precious resources keeping humans alive long after death would be a merciful relief. Storm, however, may have slowed down but he was still perfectly happy. Since my long winter-into-spring absence in Morocco he had been my constant companion. There had not even been the usual separation of the coast-to-coast Challenge. There were compromises and plans to allow this of course: the *Pennines to Highlands Walk* had become our major effort rather than trying to complete his Corbetts. He *was* failing: very deaf, going blind, walking more slowly, but still enjoying the world, and its smells. He would be 15 after all, an octogenarian in human terms.

This night, at the end of August 1990, I was woken by a crash in the vestibule. Something had bumped into the heater. I then heard Storm rubbing along the wall and into the bedroom. As he enjoyed a good rub against door frames or furniture, I simply went back to sleep again. Half an hour later there were more bumps and thumps. Half an hour later the crashing came from beside my bed, but not on the usual side for the dog. I switched on the light to find Storm stuck in the narrow passage between bed and bookcase, trying to scrabble forwards as if in a panic. I lifted him over to the bedside rug where he usually slept and he stretched out there again. An hour on I was woken by a loud crash in the vestibule and this time realised something was really amiss. Storm could not stand yet strove desperately to try and move forwards. All power and co-ordination had gone from his legs.

He had been shaking his head more of late and I wondered if the ear infection had come raging back. Or was it another, more severe stroke – which could mean the end? For the rest of the night I lay on the floor under a quilt, supporting Storm whenever these turns of frantic action came on him, giving him something to lean on, as he seemed to need in the comatose intervals. At one time, after struggling to find his feet, and failing, he looked up and gave my nose a gentle lick, a farewell gesture which had me weeping over the hapless animal in my arms.

I try hard to be a pessimist so life can only give pleasant surprises but, when it comes to facing death, we all become hopeless optimists. For a year or two I'd been thinking 'In a year or two.' Now it was suddenly 'In four hours.' In four hours I'd drive to Kirkcaldy to the vet with Storm – and be coming back alone. It was a heartbreaking prospect. Love, at the last, only has tears.

Time and again Storm struggled, driven by forces he neither knew nor understood, so all I could do was hold him tight and comfort him a little. Eventually I had to go for a pee. Storm tried to follow and scrabbled and crashed blindly into things so, when I held him again, it was long minutes before he stopped his wild panting. I nipped along to switch on the kettle but never returned to make the cup of tea. Eventually time wore on. Someone must be in the veterinary centre earlier than the official opening. We'd be there then.

Locked doors and locked motor caravan were not easy to deal with while carrying the helpless dog. I left him on the passenger seat and rushed to lock the front door. When I got back to the Transit I found he had fallen

Storm by the wintry River Tweed

off the seat and was wedged upside down, in the well of the step. He had also been sick and peed on the floor. Poor Storm. He was a fastidiously clean animal (even burrs from the garden would keep him teasing at his coat for hours) and being unable to stand would be very unpleasant, assuming he could even eat and assuming he could be nursed in the first place. No, it was all over.

We received instant attention. No hope. No arguments. It doesn't take long to fill a syringe and snip the hair from a muscular leg. I fled, driving I know not where, like a wounded animal myself, suddenly so utterly alone in strangling misery.

Sure, he was a gorgeous fella.

ONE GAME, MANY APPROACHES

The variety of hill enjoyment is something which has always attracted me. I rambled into the hills as a boy with all a boy's curiosity – and perhaps have never really grown up. But that curiosity led to trying all manner of related sports and pastimes which were hill-orientated. To me climbing, canoeing, skiing, sailing, flower-hunting, bird-watching were all means to an end, not ends in themselves; they were ways of adventuring into the wilds, of bagging Munros by more interesting, more demanding ways. I just wish I had discovered some of them earlier, added them to my young enthusiasm for wildlife and history, for the wild and lonely places of my native Scotland. So, in this section, I have gathered together various pieces which touched on the different approaches and also a few other pieces which I hope are of interest/concern to all hillgoers. We all have to face the worst foe of all, one as absent from the tourist brochures and guidebooks as are dirty-weather photographs – the eternal midge. There is also something about red deer. I would be less tolerant now, for last spring I observed a crippled, winter-poor stag on three legs. It had not been killed to put it out of its suffering as, in a few months, a 'sportsman' would pay £300 to shoot it. And they call it sport!

The Ben Nevis Observatory

If you ask any of the tens of thousands of visitors to Ben Nevis what the tumbled stones once were that now lie on the summit, only one in a thousand will know that they are the remains of the Ben Nevis Observatory, which was operational over a century ago.

The establishment of the observatory was an adventure typical of days that saw the dawn of our technical world. Robert Louis Stevenson's father, Thomas, was an engineer and lighthouse-builder, and only too practically aware of weather. He was one of the people (Lord Kelvin was another) who pushed for an observatory. He proposed a whole series of mountain stations, so that comparative studies of changes in pressure, humidity and temperature could be made. Weather forecasting as such was very new, and it is ironic that the Ben Nevis Observatory had already closed when this suddenly became very important, with the development of the aeroplane.

The Scottish Meteorological Society decided on Ben Nevis as the site for the observatory. Big but accessible, it is 'interestingly' sited in the track of Atlantic storms. Stevenson drew up plans for the building in 1879 but, with no money available, nothing happened.

Enter Mr Clement L. Wragge. 'The Inclement Rag', as he was to be nicknamed, was a lively gentleman of some character, and from 1881 to 1883 he was a perambulating observatory himself, climbing the Ben daily, leaving sea level at 4.40 a.m. being on the summit from nine to ten and getting back to sea level at 3.30 p.m. During the ascent and return he took readings at several intermediate stations. He was paid expenses, but did the work voluntarily.

In June 1983 a centenary weekend was organised in Fort William by the Royal Meteorological Society (the successor to the 'Scottish'), and Wragge's route was repeated. Seventy people left the distillery at 5 a.m., a unique event in itself, and ascended by the Livingstone Stone, the Lochan, Brown's Well and other sites, where barometers and thermometers appeared and readings were taken. The weather cleared off the summit – the spirit of Wragge in evidence? It was in light of his findings (and a deal of experience since) that it was decided that midsummer, if a bit early, was a better time to celebrate than the more accurate wildness of autumn. After all, the mean temperature during the 21 years of observatory life proved to be one degree below freezing. Were Ben Nevis a few hundred feet higher, it would have a glacier flowing from its summit.

The walk was preceded by a meeting, where a series of speakers ranged over different aspects of mountain weather. Their predecessors in knicker-bockers and with huge mercury barometers would surely have approved.

What would they have thought, though, of Wragge's three million log entries going on to a computer tape system which will allow all sorts of analytical study previously thought impossible? Meteorology has come a long way.

One speaker talked about the Cairngorm Automatic Weather Station – ironically enough, as the Ben Nevis Observatory was so expensive and complicated to operate simply because it had to be manned. Instruments could not be left outside because they iced up. There was no electronic or microchip wizardry allowing automatic records. To take hourly readings, day and night, non-stop, over the years meant a considerable residential staff.

I remember vividly my first visit to the Cairngorm summit observatory, a Heriot-Watt University project. I was sheltering in the lee of the rescue hut, in a freezing fog, when there was a click, a hum, and out of an icy drum rose a battery of instruments. I recognised an anemometer (so it was nothing 'extra-terrestrial') and realised the machine was weather-reading. After a few minutes it clicked and with a hum descended into the drum again. Quite uncanny.

On Cairn Gorm they now have a Mark II observatory functioning, with a whole battery of readings taken every half-hour and relayed back to Edinburgh. The Glasgow Weather Centre, at the press of a button, can obtain a computer read-out to assist forecasting. It is at this stage, however, that we could see history repeating itself: this observatory, too, could close down due to lack of funding from government sources.

Even Wragge's dogged work did not spur the government of his day to do more than promise £100 a year towards running costs. It did show the value of an observatory, however, and a public appeal to establish one was launched early in 1883. Queen Victoria chipped in £50. By the autumn, the building and path had been constructed, and 17 October saw the official opening.

The first superintendent was a Mr Ormond. One wonders if Wragge applied, and was passed over as too much of an individualist. (He emigrated to Australia and set up an observatory in New South Wales.) He might have found it difficult to be confined in crowded quarters, but from all we read there seemed to be a friendly and harmonious atmosphere in the observatory. The workers were, in many cases, self-funding enthusiasts (the shortage of money was always a problem). W. T. Kilgour's book, *Twenty Years on Ben Nevis* (a reprint is available, published by Ernest Press), shows them tobogganing and playing ping-pong (on a table carved out of the snow) when conditions allowed. They also skied, and went curling on the Half-Way Lochan. Royds, who was Scott's meteorologist, trained on the Ben, and Bruce, one of the staff, led the two 'Scotia' Antarctic expeditions. A young physicist, Wilson, followed up his research, inspired by the Ben, to win a Nobel Prize in due course.

They had more than their ration of snow, and after a first winter of being constantly buried by it, there was some rebuilding, including a 'conning tower' exit 30 ft up. This remained clear even when the buildings were covered over. In 1884 something like 4,000 visitors looked in, and a local hotelier erected a 'hotel' to cater for those wanting to see the sunrise on top of Britain. A toll of one shilling was charged for using the track, more if you rode up. Observers did a two-month stint on top of the Ben and then changed with a Fort William colleague. A sea-level observatory had been set up in the town to allow comparative studies. The summit was the more popular posting. Information was relayed by telegraph; then, later, by telephone. Government funds of £250 per annum were allowed for the town observatory, but the £100 a year for the summit station never altered, and it was forced to close in 1904.

Early accounts of climbing Ben Nevis, by people like W. W. Naismith and Norman Collie, often mentioned the observatory. They renamed the ravine down which rubbish was tipped Gardyloo Gully. Angus Rankin, who was once an assistant to Wragge (and superintendent at the time of the closure), climbed *down* Tower Ridge in 1895. What memories he must have had.

A broken spectre in South Castle Gully, Ben Nevis

The Harlot

Ben Nevis is a mountain
of loveless loveliness.
Like a fat woman she broods,
cold-shouldered of warm romance,
too drunken for gentle kiss.
Love has just scratched her. She reeks
like a discarded garment.

As so many cold hundreds
have pissed against the cairn,
she is soiled through and wet
and weary in her solitude.

Yet it is to this harlot
the generations come – brash boys
to test their nascent lusts,
a giggle that so often has an echoed death.

I have come to hate the bitch.
The sterile heart of her is stone
and her smile is slimy ice.
We should have heeded the old advice:
not all snowy frills – or hills – are nice.

Sunset from the CIC Hut

149

The First Munro on Skis

OSLR 51, 57

This piece was written over 30 years ago and I only rediscovered it recently – and marvelled at my zest and strength in those days. That first Munro on skis was climbed in ordinary ski equipment: no touring bindings with free heel lift, no skins, nothing to help. All that came later with ski-mountaineering in the Alps and High Atlas – but there is nothing quite like the brave confidence of youth. I have therefore left the text unaltered.

'Ya! Penguin!' jeered the faces at the back window of the mountaineering club bus as our skis went into the boot. I held my peace for I knew what they felt and said: for was it not we who christened the piste-bound players so? It chanced that we had seen films showing penguins grouped on ice floes, and, later, when rounding Cairngorm to look down on Corrie Cas, there they were – little figures on each patch of snow. With one voice the boys cried, 'Penguins!' The name stuck. As climbers we all felt superior: ours was the freedom of the hills. The mobs by the tows, what did they really know of the hills?

Alongside, though, was the thought that there should be 'real' skiing. Penguins obviously enjoyed their sport; surely it could find a place as a real mountaineering pursuit? Alpine literature told of climbs on skis and traverses over snowy ranges. Hillary had done this same sort of thing in New Zealand. At the back of our minds lay an unvoiced hope: why not in Scotland? Perhaps the crux of the feelings came when we had struggled up through deep snow to a snow-encrusted cairn above Drumochter and there followed the wild sweep of a ski track down the slopes before us. But there were few such tracks on the pages of Scottish mountaineering. A year later we bought skis and the school where we taught began to make them for the pupils.

There were no new Munros left for me to climb south of the Great Glen at weekends; rock- and ice-climbing was not always possible, so here was another possibility for our weekly winter camping and climbing trips, another (to us) side to explore of the 'great game' of mountaineering. The mountains are what matters: we were greedy to add any reason for tasting their delights again and again. But there was to be no 'penguining!'.

The harsh winter brought ski slopes to Fife and, after a first morning on a golf course, we lugged our skis up Largo Law (just under 1,000 ft). The snow was icy and crusted and as we zigzagged across the slopes we had all the thrills and spills we wanted. We sped over the tops of fences and often into gorse bushes, each run ending in a kick-turn – all we could manage – and a run in the other direction. For many days afterwards, fit climbers though we thought ourselves, we suffered aches and pains and stiffness such as we had never known. Our pupils revelled in the sufferings of their mentors.

Our next outing was to the Ochils where we camped at Paradise, above Dollar. There we slaved a morning on a good slope until the secret of turning was found. We almost made a piste, so in the afternoon two of us fled for the tops. Along with the dog we battered our way up the 2,000 ft of White Wisp, every now and then cowering as the stinging ice particles blasted across the snow. On top it was a sheer hell and we crouched long minutes gasping and blinded, stunned by the brute force of it. We went down the lip of the corrie, beyond which the debris of huge wind-slab avalanches choked the hollow of the burn. Over half a mile of circling snow had come off and as we skied along we trembled at the risk of setting off another lot. Vanishing in and out of clouds, we again zigzagged down the corrie and round the hill. The first taste of the heights was good. We must learn to turn properly though. Kick-turns only were limiting and apt to become fall-down turns.

One of two odd attempts followed and then one glorious day occurred just along from the school with new powdery snow lying six inches deep on the 100-yard brae. After our learning on rough hillsides and icy slopes it was incredible – and easy. Our feelings towards 'Penguins' mellowed. Tows have their uses! (As long as they do not become chains.) When we could fit in ten turns before arriving at the beach at the bottom we felt a glow of satisfaction and a longing for the hills again. Once more, in dreams, we re-read those entries in the Alpine huts that told of expeditions – Chamonix to Zermatt. Some day perhaps . . .

Now was the time for a 3,000-footer, the first Munro on skis. The chance came unexpectedly. Two boys together and myself separately set off to hitch north for a rendezvous on the edge of the Moor of Rannoch one Friday. On Saturday we had our eye on a new snow route and, on Sunday, when the club bus came up, the Upper Couloir of Stob Ghabhar was planned for the lads.

The farthest any of us got was Strathyre. There I spent a tentless night out on the snow in the forest; an unforgettable experience: so still that a candle stuck in the snow burned without a flicker and, cosy with a li-lo and two sleeping bags, it was a night of pure magic. The snow varied from ankle deep to over the knees, and on Saturday everything was still blocked. Until it consolidated, climbing would not be up to much. A phone call to the club secretary confirmed the bus would still go – as far as it could. Wherever it stopped there would be snow: deep, dry, powdery, made for skis. The first lift took me to Edinburgh where I caught a train home to Fife for lunch and an afternoon of local rock-climbing. Later I heard the two boys had spent the weekend camping and climbing in the Ochils.

At seven the next day the bus bore us off to Perth and along west where we got stuck at Lochearnhead: Glenogle was impossible. But what matter? I put on my skis as soon as the bus stopped. The others were all on foot, about ten of them. 'A nice rescue team if I go and break a leg!' I

Gleouraich and Sgurr a'Mhaoraich from the cairn of Creag a'Mhaim

Supernaturally snowy for skiing up Carn Liath. Creag Meagaidh beyond

thought. The Glenample track was under deep snow with one line of foot-prints winding up.

I stripped to the waist at the start to enjoy the broiling sun. Legs swung forward in turn. What climber does not revel in perfect rhythm? Here it was then: on and on up the glen, across the burn, gradually ascending and traversing the hillside. Only occasionally was a turn necessary, only occasionally a herring bone pattern to break the long clean line. Hard work it was, but joyous, satisfying. Above Glenample sheiling I heard the dogs barking and saw the dots of the climbers crossing to the cottages far below. I wondered if they could see the track high above them. Who had the laugh now?

The Allt a' Choire Fhuadaraich was crossed and for the steep climb up Creag Dubh (*the Black Crag*) I dismounted – and at once sank in to the knees. Those 500 ft are best forgotten. I had to rest continually with heart pounding furiously. Gradually I reached the stage of cursing skis and climb-ing and myself for ever putting on a pair of boots. On top of the shoulder I lay on some bare rocks with legs shaking uncontrollably and the sweat freezing my shirt tail into a board. I lay flat out, crunching sugary sweets until muscles and nerves slowly returned to normal. The others could catch up if they liked. To hell with it.

Skis on again for the continuing ascent. Several times I had to rest, twice I tried to walk only to find it even more strenuous. It went best with a slow and disciplined rhythm. Gradually the feet were gained, and spirits could do nothing but follow as Ben More and Stobinian rose over the intervening hills as great white pyramids. I kept waiting for the others to pop over the crest but they only did so as I reached the summit ridge. They must have had an even heavier time of it on foot.

The view was superlative. Lowlands and Highlands completely white-washed. I sat by the cairn eating and staring round, naming off range after range of peaks from Arran to Nevis to the Cairngorms – they were all there – all old friends, all climbed, all loved and longed for again. The Stuc had always been kind: this was the fifth perfect stay on its top in two years. I dozed off for half an hour until the cold woke me again. I fastened on the bindings and pushed off – and went flat on my back! Luckily there were no mocking pedestrians to see me. I felt a mixture of meanness and wickedness in a satisfying sort of way as I sped across Coire Chroisg to where the others were still plodding up.

After a brief exchange I swung away across the corrie again – back and forwards – long runs and sweeping turns, all with exaggerated aplomb. Some turns were not exactly smooth but I managed not to fall and spoil it all. With the others on the top ridge I swung along to Creag Dubh again. Here the slope was almost precipitous and broken by crags and frozen waterfalls and burns. Its descent was highly exciting. At the foot, long slopes of soft snow gave endless swinging routes. The air rushed past with a roaring and popping in the ears. Rather frightening. Very wonderful. Then into the banked hollow of the burn: a mild Cresta run to twist and turn down for a mile. When it became too hectic it was simple to turn up the bank and lose some momentum.

About the 1,500-ft contour I skirted round under Creagan nan Gabhar and the aim was changed to losing as little height as possible while running down Glenample. Apart from the crossing of the farm burn it was a continuous glide of one-and-a-half miles. In front lay Loch Earn and the creamy hills of Glen Ogle, behind the unwavering track from the crags and the white ridges lifted against an Alpine-blue sky: utter silence but for the soft swish of the skis; utter content; solitude yet safety; tired muscles relaxing in easy motion. Yes, every agony was worth while. I laughed and sang and then turned for a last *schuss* down into the trees and over the burn for the path again. Lingering pauses were made beside snow-ringed pools. Only a solitary hare moved in the warm hush. I walked back to the bus in a dream. Tomorrow the agony!

Three hours later the others came back. Till then I sat in the hotel enjoying cup after cup of hot, sweet tea. The armchair was soft and relaxing. The view was across to the hills we had been on. Slowly they turned pink and the shadows rose with dusk over their slopes. The first star shone out above a lemon-lined crest. At such moments we worship – and few but the mountaineer know the benediction of that long content.

Last Run: Coire na Ciste

The swing in the wind,
In the drift of snow;
Dappled delight,
Sunshine below.

The song in the heart,
In the thrust of limb,
Weaving wonder –
Sharp as a hymn

The joy of the *schuss*,
In the taste of fear,
Stolen seconds
With life made clear.

The sun in the loch –
So soon away!
Mountain mirrored
At the end of day.

The World of the Red Deer

Deer in full flight give an unmatched spectacle of graceful power. How often have we plodding climbers and walkers set them off and thought to ourselves, 'I wish I could travel as fast and effortlessly as that'?

As a schoolboy, descending from a traverse of Ben More and Stobinian, I had the odd experience of being the recipient, rather than the creator, of a deer panic. In a remnant of old forest I came on some grazing deer and quickly dropped to ground and crawled in under a small bank where I was able to stay out of sight, out of smell, and enjoy a very good look at the herd.

Slowly the deer grazed diagonally down on to my hide. The wind was strong from them to me so eventually they would scent me when they'd passed downhill. In ex-WD gear I wouldn't be seen, as long as I kept still, sitting on my hands, pale face buried in a heather clump, but those long heads that rose between rasping bites of coarse grass had twitching noses that never stopped their search for the enemy – a very efficient sort of olfactory radar.

Then on the slope above, there was a snort from a watchful hind and in a second every beast was in flight, careering down the hillside, leaping, bounding, in jerky yet fluid motion. A royal smashed past a few feet to my left, then another took a dive down my small sheltering bank, his hooves carving into the ground just a yard from my toes and spraying my legs with black peat. I made myself very small as the stags crashed down the heathery, birch-studded hillside. I suppose they'd all gone in half a minute but it seemed an eternity of fascination and fear to a cringing youth.

Deer are so much part of our hill heritage it is worth knowing a little about them. A little is all we ever know I feel, but the big danger is when we stop learning and questioning; then we become set in our attitudes and prejudices.

On one Challenge crossing of Scotland two girls (new to the hills) who were partnering me were horrified to see the spring casualty rate among deer, a mortality due to cold and wet, exhaustion and starvation. It was hardly the romantic image of red deer! If deer have a tough life it is entirely due to human history, so man has a moral obligation to look after their well-being. This obligation is not always fulfilled.

Red Deer (*Cervus elaphus*) are really forest animals, but over the centuries we have destroyed Scotland's natural woodlands and driven the deer to live in the harsh environment of the higher, exposed hills. Trees and cultivation are fenced off against their hungry assaults. They have a very lean time of it in winter, and if the spring grass does not come to their succour, they die in large numbers.

Good estates ensure there are shelter belts of trees available; they feed the deer in winter and shoot the full recommended quota to keep the numbers down to what the ground can support. People who are indignant at this 'cruel blood sport' are often quite ignorant about why deer are shot. It simply comes down to this: if deer are not culled, they die of starvation.

Shooting the extra beasts is probably the least cruel way of dealing with the problem of a stock surplus. Views on the social set-up of the 'sport' must be kept separate from the necessity of managing the deer for their own interest. There are plenty of misconceptions about the actual culling. Usually it is the weak, undersized and malformed beasts that are weeded out, not the finest, which would obviously be a self-defeating exercise.

Stalking stags is turned into a sport as an economic necessity as much as anything else. If suckers will actually pay to do the work – more fool them. But it's money that keeps a Highland economy viable. The keepers have the task of culling the hinds. Throughout, it is a case of shooting deer as cleanly as possible for their own good.

Those who go regularly on the hill become aware of the system which has evolved and tend to accept its necessity, though I would challenge many of the beliefs. I'd prefer to see the medieval, land-owning system swept away and replaced by more efficient systems, allowing more *people* to occupy the land – which was filched from them in the first place. But that is another topic – even though the deer could benefit too.

Wandering the hills for recreation is an activity of very recent origins. The 'unspoilt wilderness' many enthuse about is, in reality, nothing of the kind. We approach much of it by paths made for stalking purposes and we have easy walking surfaces because it is grazed. It would seem reasonable then, that we, as the largest users who invest least, treat the landscape with respect, and those who own it and make their living from it with fairness. Our gripes mustn't be allowed to affect the efficiency of managing deer.

In 1934–35, Frank Fraser Darling made the first intensive study of deer, and his book, *A Herd of Red Deer*, is still a valuable source book. Probably the most useful recent equivalent is Clutton-Brock and Albon's *Red Deer in the Highlands*, while a short summary is in Clutton-Brock and Ball, *Rum, the Natural History of an Island* – a book which is worth studying for the interplay of how things affect each other. Vast areas of Rum have been fenced off for a century-long experiment to re-create the natural woodland environment.

Fraser Darling and Morton Boyd's *The Highlands and Islands* is a highly readable earlier study of Highland ecology (Collins *New Naturalist* but also in paperback) which I'd make compulsory reading for every climber and hillwalker. Still easily found are the various books by Lea McNally: *Highland Deer Forest; Year of the Red Deer*, etc., which are marvellously illustrated with the author's photographs, taken as a professional stalker. The first deer book I ever met was Mortimer Batten's *The Singing Forest*. He is a largely forgotten naturalist now but this book has been reprinted several times and would be worth finding in a library to start off an interest in deer in children.

Deer stalking takes place in autumn and it is only wise to keep off areas when casual walking could spoil the cull and where we run the risk of a high-velocity bullet through our skulls. This is not really a hard self-restriction. The middle of August to the end of the third week in October is the traditional stalking period. Many estates put up notices at this time giving a local contact where enquiries can be made about where to go. (Permanent banning-notices are simply self-defeating rather than intimidating. If the public is to co-operate, it has to be offered information.)

Often there is no stalking on Sunday. Vast sheep areas are not stalked at all, and there are huge areas of lower hills where stalking does not occur. There is culling on National Trust for Scotland land such as Kintail, but public access has priority and there are no restrictions. Few islands are stalking country. Many ranges like the Cuillin or Ben Nevis are barely used for sport. Great passes like the Cairngorm lairigs are rights of way, as are many major glens. Coastal walking or following our lowland canals are good options for the stalking season. Munro-bagging should be kept in perspective, too, and the autumn semi-moratorium is no bad thing.

As I detest midges more than most things in life, leaving them to enjoy their sporting season for humans is no hardship either. By the end of October the first frosts have generally cleared away those devils, the colours are on the hill and the bellowing back in the glens.

The keepers still have to cull their set numbers of hinds and this goes on until it's done – often well into the new year. Undermanning can make the task nigh impossible on some estates; on others the approach is far too casual. The Scottish deer population is something like 50,000 too many at present, so every bad spring produces the sorry sight of dead deer. This is simply the result of bad management past and/or present. I think the system stinks.

The traditions are being eroded, too, by the repeated turnover of estates and their speculative commercial asset-stripping. Foreign and company ownership often leaves a huge gap between boss and keeper and the traditions. Sadly, the sporting sportsman is becoming rarer these days. The toffs are no longer willing to crawl about all day in the wilds. They want to be driven up, given minimal exercise, and the egoistic pleasure of shooting a wild animal. They are as out of touch with hill reality as some walkers and climbers!

The warning notices pointing out the danger of bullets are not altogether a bluff. I've twice had close encounters of a nasty kind with flying lead. As lads, ignorant about stalking, two of us hove over a horizon just as someone fired at a stag. He missed the stag. He also – just – missed us.

The other time I came near to being shot was in May, when nobody should have been firing a rifle. It was near Loch Pattack in a thick, rolling fog. I actually *felt* the blast. Almost at once the fog rolled away and in all that open bowl not a soul was to be seen. I'd gone to ground so the culprit could not have known of my presence. But nobody appeared. There were no deer. Nothing. I'm still puzzled by the incident and the local keeper

Stag at Loch Ossian Youth Hostel

could offer no likely explanation either when I told him.

Keepers are a group of people I admire tremendously. Many have to live in remote places, work long and unsociable hours (often in foul conditions), must cope with clients who are often self-indulgent and in poor physical shape, and they must have the ability to turn their hands to anything. They are invariably superb field naturalists, socially active and grand yarners. They probably live the sort of lives humans were meant to live and possess the tough, gentle content of wild things, instead of the self-inflicted urban hang-ups that create so many of the world's evils.

June is the month of deer calving. Certain corries are always favourites for dropping calves and, if known, should be avoided at that time. The long-legged, dappled calves lie alone and without movement, but the hind will always be grazing and watching not far off so, never, ever, think they are lost or abandoned and 'rescue' them. They have no fear at that stage and you may have a right old job to escape being followed. Don't touch the calf, the mother may reject it if it smells of alien human handling.

The stags' antlers are cast each year and are best left where found as they are nibbled and eaten to recycle the chemicals and nutrients needed for growing the next set, which is probably more useful than lying in the loft at home or being turned into a table lamp. The antlers grown through the summer are covered in a fur called 'velvet', which then dries and falls

Liathach from the Horns of Alligin

off, or is rubbed off by the irritable beasts. Come October, the stags are at their peak and engage in the rut – the mating game that has the hills echoing to their roaring: a sound I find utterly enthralling. To lie in a tent with stags bellowing round the hills is to touch the marvellous.

It is a sound which can be imitated fairly easily and I've brought irate stags near by issuing an apparent challenge. You don't want to tangle with rutting stags, however. They do, occasionally, attack humans at this season. On the other hand, feeding deer can make them half tame and easy to see. Tom Rigg, the warden at Loch Ossian youth hostel, can conjure stags out of Rannoch Moor by banging a bucket of food at the door.

In the summer, stags and hinds – by then in separate groups – will wallow in peat bogs for coolness and to be rid of pests such as the bot fly, which lays eggs under their skin or up their noses. The breezy summits and old snow patches will be favourite spots to lie on.

Red deer come as stags and hinds (roe deer have bucks and does) and their young are calves (not fawns). Yet just to make nonsense of pedantry, I've often heard keepers calling antlers 'horns'.

Deer have been very much part of my life, and I hope these notes have been of interest and helpful in understanding why stalking takes place. Being on the side of the deer, let me say that I become steadily more dissatisfied with the anachronistic system of Highland estates and land ownership. I think it is selfish and inefficient. That vast tracts can be bought and sold as casually as a loaf of bread is immoral. How many other countries in the world allows foreigners to buy its land like this? But then no foreigner is ever going to tell me I cannot walk on my country's hills.

I'll keep away while deer are culled – for the sake of the deer. But why should one man own all the deer? It wasn't like that in the past, till the betraying chiefs invented title deeds and laws to suit themselves – at the cost of the people who were tricked, pillaged and deported.

One estate recently had the press along on a PR day and, among other things, pointed out how vital the estate was to the district. They boasted that the estate supported 15 people and that the village shop would not survive otherwise. Two hundred years ago the estate's area supported 500 people, and everyone had venison as a right. And there weren't too many deer, so the poor beasts didn't starve through mismanagement and maladministration!

It is high time politics entered into this subject. The present government has been shown to be as 'green' as porridge and conservationists and bureaucrats alike fight shy of a battle royal. Maybe it's time we began to roar like stags in the rut. Deer deserve a better deal.

In the Rut

The summer pipers have flickered
wings off to Africa
their singing spent.
Only a penny robin limps a tune
on a garden wall –
pallid reminder of the lusts of spring,
green season of the birds.

Red autumn belongs to antlered hearts,
who woo through rain and frost
and snow their passion on the hills.
What toys birds are when stags roar
and roar their month-long rage
of thunderstorm
and waterfall
combined.

There is a remnant of respect
in our plastic observation
of sinewy beast.
Stags have the power to gralloch our past
and remind us of heathery origins
and cave man doubts.
They are our hoary past breathing clouds
of frosty fear into the clean air
we live without.

Stags are the nearest to gods we have,
the nearest to the oldest
stalking hopes of man.
When we hear them bellow on the open strath
we are shut in to centuries
forgotten, rutting the generations
up to now
till we stand in all-modern pride,
antlered with self-congratulation
at our species.

I would have stayed a stag.

Looking to Knoydart over the Sound of Sleat

The Menace of Midges

There are few things which merit universal detestation. *Culicoides impunctatus* certainly has no savoury reputation in its favourite territory of Scotland. Its Latin tag has a ring to it which is entirely appropriate.

The genus *Culicoides* actually has some 900 species, a nightmare statistic were the vast majority not decently docile. They range from the Arctic to the Caribbean, and the first Everest expedition in 1921 complained of being bitten viciously at nearly 14,000 ft. *C. impunctatus* is not found above 10,000 ft, which is not really a comforting statistic on the Cuillin Ridge or Ben Nevis. It also tends to avoid strong sun and any wind: the last tendency being of vital importance in the months of summer savagery.

Normally in Scotland we play a game of finding a sheltered spot for pitching a tent. In summer the necessity is to find a dry and blessedly breezy knoll. Earlier I mentioned camping on a spur above the gorge of a burn coming off Ben More on Mull. It caught a breeze beautifully, yet just a few yards off there was a sun-glittering haze of midges filling the sheltered trough of the stream. You could plunge an arm into this dancing porridge of midges and see pink skin change to grey as thousands of midges latched on, then, on withdrawing the arm, they would fall away again. It was a fascinating game, but at the back of our minds was the thought 'God help us if the wind drops!'.

Most of the 40–50 species of British midges persecute sheep, deer and horses, even hens and ducks, rather than *Homo sapiens*, but a few do favour sucking human blood. There is no sex equality among these devils. It is the female that bites. She does this to stock-up on blood which is needed for developing her eggs. The female midge has a powerful mouth for its minute size, with which it saws its way into our skin, injects saliva to ensure a good blood supply, then sucks the blood up through its food tube. By the time we notice the bite it is probably too late for prevention. We can only swipe with a curse and bear the itch. Scratching just makes the irritation worse, but restraining from scratching is not very easy. Restraint is rewarded by the irritation slowly fading away, while scratching leads to greater irritation and often a recurrence of the itch 24 hours later.

Midges become active by June and will be present until the frosts of autumn bite. They are abundant in boggy areas in the Highlands where sphagnum moss, rushes and damp predominate. They seem to love rhododendron jungles and I've never forgotten Glen Etive nights of misery when our party eventually fled to seek sanctuary in Glencoe youth hostel.

Midges go through the stages of egg, larva, pupa and adult insect. When you think of the millions of acres of boggy land in Scotland, it is not surprising that there are such huge numbers of midges. A week to ten days sees midge eggs hatch and they then spend about ten months in the larva stage, when they are quite omnivorous. The pupa stage lasts less than a fortnight and then the flying insect is with us. Both males and females feed on nectar and the female will quickly develop and lay up to 70 eggs. They don't actually need a meal of our blood to do this (after all there are not so many humans per acre in our boglands), but to produce further eggs they do need a blood boost. One reason tourists see so few deer in the summer is that the deer have fled to the heights in order to escape being victimised. (There is more chance of wind higher up.)

Considering the misery midges cause to humans in the Highlands, and how vociferously this is expressed, I am puzzled by the lack of historical references to *C. impunctatus* before, say, the time of Queen Victoria. Her journal describes a picnic in Sutherland in 1872 being made a misery by their attentions. Cycling to Kylesku just after the war when the road down to the ferry was being tarred, I noticed the roadmen were given time off when the midges became beyond endurance. There *were* midges (an ancient Gaelic saying suggested they were the one thing to rival Clan Campbell in their predations!) but the references are few and far between. I would like to hazard that they increased in number dramatically in the late eighteenth and early nineteenth century as people were cleared from the glens and their cultivated acres reverted to wet as the sheep grazed the goodness out of the land.

In more practical terms, nobody has really come up with a solution to the problem. As a lad I can remember a great blowing of trumpets by the Scottish Tourist Board, who were sponsoring confident research into ways of eradicating the midge. Many million million midges on, we are still suffering.

Insect-repellents are the best we can do, faced with the near impossible task of changing the wet desert we have created. It is probably a case of the sins of our fathers being vented on their children's children! All kinds of herbs, oils and chemicals have been tried over the years. In Norway I have used a light bee-keeper's veil as a protection against Arctic mosquitoes, and have not hesitated to don it in Scotland since. Basically, I just take care not to be caught. Camping high or on a col is essential. If the weather is midge-perfect I'd sooner go home.

Perhaps Skye is the place most people recall for their worst midge experiences. A warm, moist evening without a ripple on Loch Brittle can see the camp site reduced to a scene more reminiscent of the Crimean War than of people supposedly enjoying a holiday in the hills. Figures crouch over fires of driftwood and seaweed, or are sealed up in sweat-box tents nearly asphyxiated by smoke-coils, while now and then someone will dash for the distant toilet block wearing mitts and a balaclava! Under those circumstances I move. Walking provides only temporary respite. Even on top of Sgurr Alasdair, the devils are waiting to renew their assault. If transport is available I'll move to wherever there is a breeze or to the shelter of a hut, hostel, B-and-B or anything else.

Every few years there is a new insect repellent on the market claiming to be the answer. Discounting the hyperbole of the advertising, there certainly has been considerable improvement. Relief – even temporary relief – is always welcome.

The Gaelic for midge, *Meanbh-chuileag*, means 'little fly' (a surprisingly moderate term for a language rich in irony), but even generations of living in the Highlands does not give any additional immunity. Some people suffer more than most. Some, poor creatures, are allergic to midge bites. None I've met claims immunity.

Some time ago there was quite a correspondence in a newspaper about midges and one lady propounded the prophylactic of strong vitamin C tablets. She had read about this and tried the idea. 'It works splendidly,' she claimed. Would readers like to try this some time and let us know the results – or any other remedy or defensive tactics?

All creatures are supposed to have a place in nature's scheme of things, but this theory perhaps meets its Waterloo faced by the ranks of *Culicoides impunctatus*. I don't think the world would fall apart with the eradication of the midge. Not enough is known about the early stages of *Culicoides*. The larvae may provide a vital form of food for some other insect (probably noxious too) but the fully grown insects are not a major food-supply, except perhaps for our insectivorous plants – butterworts and sundews. Fish, frogs and birds may eat a few.

The midge is rich in nitrogen and the sundews and butterworts do need them. Both these flowers have leaves sticky enough to hold midges (but nothing much bigger), which are then sucked of their nourishment. When you see the starfish-like butterworts crawling out of the peat pools you can be sure the midge season is about to commence.

Chemical warfare on midges in the field has proved impracticable, for any spray that would kill midges would kill beneficial insects as well. Altering the environment is effective but too expensive to be practical on the scale we need. Perhaps the only benefit from the yearly midge plague is that it keeps the swarms of holidaymakers within bounds. Without *Culicoides impunctatus* the Highlands would be overrun by *Homo sapiens*.

Joking apart, the midge is not just a Scottish phenomenon. England, Wales, Ireland and Northern France share *impunctatus*, though there is some evidence for separate races. Think of it – nationalistic midges!

I've only met one instance of midges proving beneficial. In Iceland they reach such vast numbers and produce several generations in the long-lit summer, that a film of the dead ones will cover pastures to such an extent that they act as an enriching fertiliser. The grass round Myvatn is certainly green enough. I was lucky to be there between the midge-million periods and, walking through the farmlands, saw cows with peculiar leather harnesses round their bellies. Enquiry discovered that these were trusses to hold up the cows' huge udders, so well-fed were they on the midge-manured grass!

A last Skye anecdote. At one midge-infested camp site a plaintive Braehead voice wailed from a tent. 'What can I do? What can I do? The midges are driving me mad!'

From the tent next door came the calm suggestion, 'Open the door, Jock, and let them out.'

The Cairngorms from Strathspey

LASTLY

I grew up with my particular Munro's Tables *listing 277 Munros (276 plus Tarsuinn) so the ups and downs of revisions over the years, in which I had a minor part, always meant fresh sorties to top-up the personal list. This lament was compounded, personally, by having several rounds to top up but was usually helped by most of the changes being to hills which were next to old friends or were splendid Corbetts being promoted – all of which I tended to have climbed several times already.*

In 1990 came the 'hare' of Foinaven and I was asked to make comments on the situation. That piece ends this collection but first I have added some pieces concerned with how we behave or have behaved and how it affects the future. If there is much future. We can talk the Cairgorms to death as well as trample them into oblivion. We can only muddle through for so long then, like a glissade, we pass the stage of being able to stop. What price Munros when we have used up all the world's resources?

Over the Top

A book review of mine in *The Great Outdoors*, which looked warily on mountain bikes and books about them, brought a number of letters ranging from complete agreement to complete disagreement, which just goes to show that you cannot please all the people all the time. Truth usually lies somewhere in the middle. I am not anti-bike, being an oldie who's taken bikes into wilds all my life. Usually oldie bikes.

My feelings about bikes are thus very much middle of the road, if that is the right term. It is the extremes that I feel need to be looked at, along with the cynical exploitation which applies not only to biking, but right across the range of outdoor activities.

The sort of thing I find objectionable is the use of the Loch an Eilein area for championship bike games. The area is normally full of 'No Cycling' notices, being famed for its quietness, and resorted to for gentle walking. All this is instantly forgotten, though, when there is the chink of profit in the Aviemore coffers. A no-bikes area suddenly becomes host to bikers from all over the world.

All my early explorations of the Highlands were made by bike and hike, first with family, then alone, or with like-minded enthusiasts. Cycling, for me, has always been part of the enjoyment of the wilder parts of Scotland, as are walking, climbing, skiing, canoeing and so on.

Sadly, in all these pursuits, commercial interests have moved in. Mountain bikes are just the latest to be given the works. A few years ago I went on a canoe trip with a young student who had all the very latest gear, including a very expensive touring canoe. Mine was a 30-year-old canvas kit job, but it had taken me all the places this young tyro was to go in the next few years. I was appalled to find that his canoe actually weighed more than mine.

Walkers are constantly told they have super lightweight gear these days, but often their packs are considerably heavier than my loads of ex-WD kit when a boy. Many of the walkers I see on the West Highland Way are vastly over-equipped with rucksacks designed for the Himalaya, massive boots with Yeti gaiters, circus clothing – walking examples of the great con.

It seems now you cannot go climbing even an easy route without jangling gear suitable for the Eiger and, naturally, wearing pants in emerald, marigold and puce. You cannot walk, or visit the pub, without the latest, jargon-glutted, £250 jacket – and, of course, you wouldn't be seen dead with any old boneshaker of a bike on the hills. It has to be the gaudiest, state-of-the-art model, even if a mortgage is needed to buy it. This hype and commercial rip-off obviously works extremely well. What a brain-washed, manipulated, pathetic people we are to be led like this up the mountain path!

The mountain-bike concept is good. I'm not denying that. What I do object to is the manipulative exploitation of such blatant commercialism. Let me draw another parallel. A few years ago there was a huge commercial push to sell 'new' concepts in touring skis (the Scandinavians have been using them for 2,000 years!) which saw thousands of pairs sold. Most have stayed in attics. I have an older pair, bought and used in Norway, in the right conditions. In Scotland I have the odd day on them at best.

I once traversed the Aonach Eagach in winter with two septuagenarian members of the Scottish Mountaineering Club. We had the basics of ice axe and crampons, rope, and a couple of slings, yet many others, especially the young, were festooned with unnecessary gear, which was actually holding them back. There is a distinct indication that the young take the latest gear to mean safety, a dangerous fallacy. Youngsters believe they must have all the latest, most expensive kit. If you don't follow fashion you are an outcast. How the high priests of Mammon must laugh.

Biking has fallen into the same trap, for there are many fallacies here, too. Many of the lauded advances are not really new at all: broad tyres, lots of gears, lightness, etc. My old folding bike has broad tyres, and I can recall trying out fancy gears decades ago. Lightness is just not possible if there is real strength, unless it is obtained at the cost of leaving off other useful bits of bike, such as carriers, and mudguards.

I constantly see bikers wearing big rucksacks because they have no carriers, yet these are bikes for long journeys with much necessary equipment. There are no mudguards, yet they are being used in muddier, dirtier ground than usual. So, for the outlandish price, you have these built-in deficiencies as well.

The high prices, ironically, are an added attraction. I remember seeing a TV interview with an American female who complained she was on her second vacation to Scotland that year, when she really didn't care for travel at all. When asked why she came, the reply was, 'Oh, I've got to go twice to show I can afford it.'

There is a similar aspect with mountain bikes, skis, canoes and all the rest, an objectionable cash-induced swank. Nobody who's anybody can appear on the ski slopes in last year's fashions! I can recall when duvet jackets came in. Everyone wore them to the pub! You'll see a hundred mountain bikes in Fort William for every one in the Fannichs. Most people buying or hiring these bikes, specially designed for rough stuff, have no intention of ever doing anything rough or energetic with them, but they are 'what everyone has'. Thus the sheep are led to the commercial slaughter.

My main criticisms of books for bikers stands. Areas such as the severely eroded Lairig Ghru, the West Highland Way with its walkers, quiet Loch an Eilein, the tops of mountains, are not the place for bikers (or even walkers in many cases). The person who did all the Munros by bike may have performed a feat, but so did the person who pushed a bed from Land's End to John o' Groats. These ploys proved little about bikes, or beds.

Loch Treig from one of the 'new' Munros, Beinn Teallach

I can already hear the interjection, 'But who are you to talk, having done so much many times over?' Which is precisely why I have some authority to speak. I've done a lot of it, for a long time, whether it is walking, climbing, ski-touring, or biking. Climbing all the Munros is a natural continuation of walking up one of them – using a bike isn't. The bike equivalent is Patagonia to Alaska or round the world. On the Munro trip, when I hit long road miles, not the place for walking, I swopped to bike, using it in its natural place. Cycling Munros or walking roads are extremes; sanity lies in the middle somewhere.

In Scots law a push-bike is 'an aid to pedestrianism' and so can be taken over rights of way. A mountain bike can be a great aid to pedestrianism, shortening long approaches, long miles of tar or forest dullness, gaining time for other things. It can give superb tours away from the hazards of vehicles. It is a true part of exploring the wilds.

My plea is to tread softly in the wilderness. There is no need to go in screaming colours which show a disregard for the very landscape being used. The mountains have rights, too. They are more important than all our selfish little games on them. It is our duty – in the wilds – to be unobtrusive, to blend, to assimilate something of its tenor. When the ptarmigan play ghetto-blasters, so may we. When the deer wear emerald, marigold and puce, so may we.

The summit of Linthach in winter

Protected Out of Our Own

My interest is mainly with mountains, and having travelled and climbed in scores of countries, I have no hesitation in placing Scotland's mountain heritage high on any list. In how many countries in Europe for instance could you hike for a week and not meet anyone? Wilderness is a resource and a very fragile one. Our important Scottish wilderness is dwindling fast – as fast in fact as the growth of bodies set up to protect it.

In the last few years all the western glens south of Glen Shiel have been developed. The bulldozers have ploughed through them all, either to create geometric forestation or plant those power lines to Skye. It is disturbing that one glen was planted by the then chairman of the Scottish Countryside Commission who is a well known conservationist!

North of Loch Maree Colonel Whitbread for many years maintained a policy of discouraging visitors to his land, this being done in the name of preserving a precious wilderness. Yet he suddenly ups and sells it – to a caring Dutchman it chanced, but Arab, German, Yank, it does not matter which, except it can happen. There is no security, no continuity, it could have been a barrel of beer sold. Some caring!

It would seem there are two reasons for landowning: to make money (or vice versa) and/or for rather selfish fun, based on exclusiveness and wealth. Money, sadly, seems to be able to overcome scruples every time. Lack of genuine, disinterested, public control over our landscape lies at the heart of all our weaknesses. If you or I want to build a shed in the garden, we have a system of control to go through but these people, owning what is beyond price, can buy and sell it, bulldoze it, plant it, destroy it, at whim or fancy, with no regard to the residents or the public at large. Until this is dealt with we are merely toying with symptoms not dealing with the disease, plastering boils say, instead of dealing with the blood. It is something government is good at not doing. We have a National Health Service dealing with the sickening results of smoking, but not the root cause, cigarettes. They give cash as the reason of course but this is probably fallacious. The tax on cigarettes probably merely covers the cost of treating the cancer it causes. The National Health Service was to make us healthy. Has it? Or has it just shifted the types of illness? We set up body after body to deal with the landscape, the environment, and still we see it withering away, which is not surprising when the most basic controls are missing.

Our landscape could be far better treated than it is: it could produce more, support more people, give more pleasure and for these reasons, never mind the political ones, the system needs to be changed. The big political parties seem content to leave the present inefficiencies. Legislation is invariably urban orientated.

The landowners are a powerful lobby and well organised, while those employed in the feudal system are weak and powerless. The powerful have created deserts and want to keep it so. As a mountaineer I often shock my loyal compatriots by declaring that Ireland's hills are finer than ours, because they rise, not from our desert, our destroyed landscape, but from a green patchwork of fields, stitched with hedgerows, dotted with cottages, the turf reeking like a warm blanket, and full of the sounds of life. It is the landscape as it might have been in Scotland; as it still could be, lived in, yet losing nothing of its natural beauty.

To save part of our mountain heritage some fine chunks of it were bought for the National Trust for Scotland. The spirit (and the purse) behind this was Percy Unna and he laid down stringent guidelines based on doing as little as possible to these areas, i.e. keeping man's handiwork out. The NTS seem to be, government-like, stating and agreeing to a policy – and then doing something different. Every mountain property has been 'developed': visitor centres, carparks, toilets, paths, all *creating* the very pressures they were supposed to avoid. The only paint-marked route to a mountain summit went to the top of Ben Lawers and there a plaque specifically pin-pointed the presence of rare flowers! There was a corrie on Liathach which had taken generations of use with no obvious wear and tear. It was then cairned and within a couple of seasons a gouged path was made.

Stack Polly (not NTS) had difficult access because there was no easy parking for cars: so they built a carpark, and now they have had to concrete the erosion on the mountain. It seems that bodies cannot stop behaving like this. Parkinson's Law becomes Parkinson's Disease. They must spend their budgets, write their reports, create vital statistics, and all keep their jobs secure; while seen to be doing good. It is like something out of 'Alice in Plunderland'.

At one AGM of the Scottish Rights of Way Society a couple of self-styled 'planners' put forward a motion to alter the annual report's mere noting of the proposed 'Borders' Way' to a comment of praise and encouragement instead. This was rejected by a big majority. Talking to them afterwards, I was struck by their sorrowful mystification at the outcome. Perhaps if the bureaucrats came down from their ivory towers more often and met the people they would find out some truths. The Scottish Sports Council regularly sends apologies to the Mountaineering Council of Scotland's AGM – then wonders why, when it pontificates on climbing matters, it is shot down. The Scottish Countryside Commission's idea of a 'Grampian Way' through the main Cairngorms cost thousands of pounds before its mammoth report was made public, yet a bit of consultation with the users would have shown its impracticality immediately. The protectors must stop protecting us out of our own.

There is really no call, for instance, for the Southern Uplands Way. There is nothing to stop anyone with a bit of initiative going and walking it now. It seems a British disease that we must run things for the benefit of the

Rowan berries

inefficient, the unimaginative, the lazy, as if to hasten in some gormless sheep society. It is not a Scottish tradition or desire to have waymarked routes, a system which is now seen as damaging in more enlightened countries. As most of our planners have been bred or trained south of the border, the usual time lag is only bringing these errors upon us now. We cannot even sin efficiently.

Everything must be reduced to a lowest common denominator as quickly as possible. They cannot see that if you remove all difficulty (paint the routes, introduce wardens, etc.) and remove all danger (blow up the Bad Step, ban rock-climbing, etc.) then you will have removed mountaineering. I wonder, on the broader scene, how many a Robert Burns, or Andrew Carnegie or David Livingstone we have smothered with softness? What I find peculiarly sad is the lack of imagination in so much of this.

At the head of Glen Feshie a bulldozed track has been ripped across a steep slope of alluvial deposits which was held in place by heather. Now it looks like a scree slope and the track has been washed away in places. It was so obvious, yet . . . Loch Tulla from the main road beyond Bridge of Orchy is a splendid view, but enjoy it while you can, a few years from now all you will have is a close look at a wall of conifers . . . Those pylons to Skye; did they put them through a glen with pylons already (Carron), or through a glen with a noisy main road and an obtrusive quarry (Glen Shiel)? No, they chose the one route where there was nothing of man, *because* there was nothing of man.

The machinery of planning permission is already in existence (we petty men go under its huge legs often enough); is it too much to hope that some government some day will rise above petty greed and selfish interest and ensure all changes in landform and use have to be thoroughly tested?

I am not against changes. I want to see more people living in our empty hills, as they do in Ireland without damaging the quality of the landscape; what I want stopped is the sudden changes or plans which are always sprung on the public, without warning, at the eleventh hour, whether by planners or bodies or landowners or anyone else who has a chance of affecting the shrinking wilderness. So very often the best course would be to do nothing, or little. It is like arranging flowers: so easy to go beyond the deft touch of simplicity and overload and kill the beauty intended. We overkill with kindness.

Sadly, there does not seem to be much hope in the education of youngsters. They are in the hands of the busybodies as well. Education has taken to the hills too, building its own empire, writing codes and rules, dreaming up centres and training schemes. it is a phoney set-up, but powerfully established. Mountaineers seem to be unaware of the dangers. No other sport has such interference from outsiders. Could you imagine the educationists telling the Football Association how to run things? I cringe when I hear phrases like 'simulated adventure' or 'promoting a wilderness experience'. I was in this game myself. At one time when I was feeling depressed with it all I was told, 'Cheer up, Hamish, in a year or two you'll have an assistant and be really established.' At a meeting of the Scottish Mountain Leadership Training Board I once heard one educationist happily tell another he had been made into a department and this would be another £500 a year! We do well to be cynical.

I have had my fill of this but, luckily, I have the hills to escape to. It still is very beautiful, despite all we have done to it. Surely it is worth preserving for our children. Many years ago somebody said to me that they always judged people by their attitude to trees. I once stopped a meeting which was arguing to no good end and asked round the table: 'When did you, personally, physically, plant a tree?' The answers were very revealing.

When did you last plant a tree?

Scotland – the Rot

The endless debates on conservation, access and everything else to do with the hills are, under the present system, a waste of time. It is like listening to an endless replay or a record stuck in a groove. Useless labour. What we need is not yet another tune, but to smash the bloody record player. Scotland has been emasculated (which might explain the squeaky voice), and is therefore impotent in dealing with its own destiny.

This is politics of course, and everyone bends over backwards, sideways, and stands on their head to avoid trying to introduce politics into problems, which is why the overall position does not change. Munro-baggers (Munro-haters too) are no better than cone-gatherers. The constant talking and compromising merely keeps the record turning. Scotland has been taken over and is controlled by an external power just as surely as were the Baltic States or Poland. Then they stood up and said No. Scotland doesn't, and now is the only country in Europe which has no say in its own affairs. What good is our utter rejection of England's ruling party at the polls when their interests still prevail?

We are constantly told how dependent Scotland is, how much we gain by union. If this was true, why is England so reluctant to be free of us? It's damned lies of course. Scotland is a useful place for fiscal experiments or dumping the world's nuclear waste or asset stripping our resources. We're written off politically, a lost cause, so what the hell? Could you imagine the Mar Lodge saga dragging on as it did had the estate been in an English marginal constituency? We are treated with condescension. Which is all we deserve, however. We've been cajoled, bribed or hammered into subservience for hundreds of years now. Scotland is a myth.

What other country in Europe allows its landscape heritage to be bought and sold, neglected and misused, by all and sundry? Hillwalking in the wilds is not a right, as in most countries, and only exists because we make it so. Perhaps we should make it more so? At the end of the twentieth century what place is there for the medieval landowner set-up that exists? Over vast tracts of the Highlands the land is in a poorer state now than it was a century ago.

One year the Scottish Landowners Federation hosted a press gathering at Ardverikie on Loch Laggan to put over their point of view. It was then we were told, as if it were meritorious, that the estate was vital for the local good. Didn't it support 15 families? As, two hundred years ago, it supported maybe five hundred, who's fooling who? My cynically made suggestions on several money-spinning lines brought truth to the surface. 'Do you really think that would be suitable for our ambience?' That weekend probably did the landowners more harm than anything before or since. A publication by the owner, a triple-barrelled name, bore his home address – in the English midlands. The present set-up, far from being indispensable, is a waste of resources, of *the* most precious resource mankind acknowledges – land. (Only 'God' is responsible for more wars than 'land'.) The system has failed. If they could, right now half the present landowners in Scotland would sell up. They know it doesn't work. There wasn't exactly a rush to buy the Mar estate, was there? The government's failure on that issue will never be forgotten, or forgiven.

Big landowning is an historical obscenity. The land was filched from the people in the first place, for originally land-owning didn't exist – people did. But clan chiefs, like the power-grabbers ever since, were quite happy to switch people for cash. They invented title deeds, declared themselves to be landowners, by sleight-of-hand put this over as quite legal and got to work clearing off the people from their glens – which have been misused deserts ever since. The system stinks.

It particularly stinks when we see an estate like Mar allow buildings like Derry Lodge (and many others) to rot away in emptiness, some of our finest woodlands die of neglect, or Arabs not only stop car access to the Falls of Glomach but clear all the homes in the glen there. The owners being foreign is really a side issue (some of our few really caring owners are foreign), but what outsiders do can often be worse because they know nothing of the history and traditions of Scotland.

The system is rotten, depending on foreign richness or institutional investment, neither of which is very aware of Scottish traditions, of our moral right to roam our country. Or is it blatant speculation as we've seen with the asset-stripping of Knoydart. In no case is the land improved for the land's sake, for the future good of the country itself. The government has done nothing to stop this waste of people and land, but then it is more given to rhetoric than reality.

Apart from its obtrusive jaundice-coloured signs, I've a good deal of praise for Atholl Estates. There the population has increased and the landscape has improved. Estate taxation should be geared to such improvements, with generous rebates for each additional family or new home or industry – and fierce penalties or confiscation for those who do nothing except perpetuate their own gracious living at the price of continuing decay. Or perhaps the whole system should be done away with?

Deer have to be controlled, but couldn't smallholders and farmers do that as efficiently as under the (unpeopled) present system? I know of a keeper denied a wee garden in a remote glen because it would take one acre of 30,000 acres available for grazing deer. A hundred people owning these 30,000 acres would be more commercially viable – and the land loved and lived in.

Should second homes be permitted at all? Whether it is of an estate mansion house or a wee holiday home, the absentee owner is a curse to permanent settlement. There is no moral or commercial justification for them. Only when people live in their houses, on their own acres, permanently, is there real commitment. The rest is playing – as if our heritage

On the summit of Seana Bhraigh

was a toy! Trouble is, everyone joins in. Half the Creag Dhu, never mind half the SMC, have second homes in Speyside now. The angry young men of my youth now flit from committee to committee in the endless whirl of bureaucracy's rotating disc. Conservation becomes a comfy living not a crusade; pre-recorded messages instead of furious creation.

Which is why matters return to my original contention that this is all wind on the crags until we have revolution. I can't see it happening, though. The majority are too cosy, too selfishly indulgent to vote, either in the ballot box or with their bodies before the Whitehall tanks. Maybe I was over-generous in my initial picture. It is not a record player we need to smash but a tape recorder. The machine is at the wrong speed anyway and the tape is being chewed up inside. Scotland is just a useless brown ribbon shimmering on the breeze, hanging from an alien English oak.

Pity Poor Foinaven

The frenetic atmosphere that now grips Munro-bagging was made all too apparent with the news that Foinaven might be over the magical 3,000 ft height. Throwing a juicy bone into a compound of starved dogs would have created a gentler stir. An unedifying spectacle. It is high time Munro-baggers grew up and treated the hills with a bit of respect, aye, and reverence, instead of a stage for greedy ego-boosting.

I know the reaction to this already: 'Who is he to talk? Worse Munroist of them all. Even did them in a single trip and wrote a book about it.' True enough but quite beside the point. My concern is with how we do things, with 'style', and I think on that matter we are sinning and going astray.

The Munros aren't just being climbed. They are being bludgeoned.

With the hills offering such a wide spectrum of activity, only to Munro-bag, as so many now do, is a sad waste of resources, both human and environmental. What lack of imagination not to want to know something about the flowers that line our eroded paths, to understand something of the geological structure of our worn-out landscape, to look sympathetically on the peopled past and the blows of history.

As one of Scotland's grandest hills, Foinaven needs no designation. It will stay the same, aesthetically, with or without any listing. Those only now pricking-up their ears about Foinaven or planning its ascent simply prove my point. Foinaven would be rapidly demeaned by Munro status – as happened with Beinn Teallach, as half-happened with Beinn Dearg in Torridon or Sgurr a' Choire-bheithe in Knoydart.

The rush is on for these borderline hills at the first hint of any likely promotion. Somehow they all seem to be rather fine hills which, to me, means they should have been climbed long ago by anyone knocking about the Scottish hills. If people genuinely explored Scotland for good ploys, not just for list-ticking, they would not be planning commando raids to top up the silly 'done-'em all' tally.

Much of the furore over the last big changes to *Munro's Tables* was because people were actually having to go and climb something extra, a strange grudge from those supposedly going into the hills for fun! The Mullach on Liathach was typical: howls of rage yet, had the natural and best day been taken for 'doing' the traverse of the mountain, there would have been no problem.

I was once rather peeved with a promotion, not because it made any difference to my own Munro-bagging position, but because of the timing. It was just after completing my Munros in a single trip that Sgurr nan Ceannaichean was upped to Munro-status. And I'd skipped it on the walk!

I'd passed not far from the top but diabolical weather made it not worth the risk and I curved-off downwards to Glenuig.

Had it been a Munro I would have crawled to its summit – and therein lies one of the dangers of Munro-bagging. Fanatics who have driven from Birmingham to bag a specific Munro over a weekend are not keen to be put off, and many a rash escapade is happening because of the irrational grip of Munroitis. There are plenty of alternatives to a foul day on a Munro – but blindness is an early symptom of the disease. The Munros-in-one trip was in 1974 so my attitude and comments have not changed, as anyone reading *Hamish's Mountain Walk* can note for themselves. If I am shriller now it is simply because where one could laugh off the few fanatics in the past, today's situation is no longer a joke.

Scottish Mountaineering Club ancients had long spotted that the Ordnance Survey were hazy on the country north of Loch Maree, but the OS has always given an image of infallibility and resisted outside help. It took half a century for them to admit Tarsuinn was over 3,000 ft. Later on Beinn a' Chlaidheimh slipped in too.

It is still less than a decade ago that a hill, in the middle of Perthshire, 'grew' by several hundred feet, the true delineation only appearing on the Second Series Landranger map. If the big 1984 changes were annoying to Munroists, pity the poor Corbett-bagger who suddenly found nearly a score added to the list.

Those major changes in 1984 were a mix of duty-corrections resulting from map changes and a desire to iron-out the worst anomalies – as Sir Hugh Munro himself always planned. Those who yell 'hands-off' don't seem aware that there have always been changes and revisions. The 1984 changes were made at the behest of the SMC, the keepers of the Tables and, like most compromise jobs, pleased nobody.

The vital height for Munro status is 914 metres plus. The detailed decimal factor is ignored on maps, the heights being rounded up or rounded down to the nearest metre, which is much less accurate than measuring in feet, assuming the survey height is accurate. A hill of 914 metres is not automatically a Munro. In the case of Beinn Dearg (Torridon) the decimal place saw the hill left as a worthy Corbett rather than being bastardised into a Munro; in the case of Beinn Teallach it meant elevation from peaceful Corbett to undignified Munro.

The piece published in a national newspaper publicising that Foinaven might be a Munro was irresponsible, especially during the stalking season, and it would have been far more seemly to have passed news of the possibility on to the SMC and leave them to sort it out with the OS. That such crass journalistic hype now attends the innocuous pastime of wandering up Scottish hills is sad but perhaps symptomatic of the unsacred times.

My Munro-indulgence was fortuitous rather than planned. I just happened to spend the most active years of my life permanently in the hills, usually with gangs of enthusiastic youngsters who, while keen Munro-baggers (and keen on lots of other things too), could never, ever, be so tiresomely serious as adult Munro-baggers today. It was fun, first and last.

Two of my keenest lads, my dog and I once reached the summit of the Spidean of Liathach when it still enjoyed the easy-to-remember altitude of 3,456 ft and found another man reclining at the cairn. He began to expound all about Munros to the two 14-year-olds. Munros, to them, were a private game and they didn't quite know how to react, till it was too late anyway. They then paid out just enough rope to ensure the man hung himself.

'You see, boys, this is a very special day for me. This is my fiftieth Munro. Some day when you're older I'm sure you'll find it a healthy pastime. Do you know how many you've done?'

He looked at Derry who put on his best dead-pan face to mutter, 'Hunner and twa.'

There was an almost imperceptible pause then the man quickly turned to Ali. 'And you?'

Ali smirked. 'Och I've just done hunner and three.'

Incredulity, then shock, could be read in the man's face. He quickly pointed to the dog, smirking, 'And what about him?'

I'm afraid we all burst into laughter before Ali choked out, 'Aw him, he's done them all.' The man packed up rather hastily and scurried off. Derry grinned, 'Just as well he didna ask you, Hamish.'

It is a question I've learnt to dodge fairly effectively but once I enjoyed letting the cat out of the bag. I was alone in Garth youth hostel except for two young lads who went about cooking, and everything else, with the quiet efficiency of much practice. (Busy scribbling to meet a deadline, I was not being sociable though I was observing!) Later I came on them in the dorm, with maps spread on the beds, planning their days ahead, and was soon drawn into the easy chat of hillgoers everywhere.

The conversation ranged over many places and topics and they showed a remarkable knowledge – and interest – on many matters. Eventually 'Munros' came up and I could see the inevitable looming.

'We've done about 150 Munros. How many have you done?'

I grinned back (thinking of the bloke on Liathach), 'Two thousand three hundred and eleven' – or whatever it was.

There was a silence then one yelped, 'You must be Hamish Brown' and he dived into his rucksack to produce a well-worn copy of my Munro book. 'We take this everywhere. It's great for telling you everything.'

That was probably the prettiest compliment I've had for the book, but it was also testimony to them. They liked the book because of all sorts of things and not just as a 'how-to' guide. Their interests were wide. Their love was of the hills, Scotland whole, for itself, and not just for their little games – which was marvellously refreshing. That I feel, is how Munros should be, just a part of an endless game of discovery, not an end in itself, not a blinkered obsession, not the only activity in the hills.

Pity about Foinaven. One of the grandest hills in Scotland. Now it will be worth avoiding for a year or so to miss the mobs. However, with luck, they will wear down its stony crest to below the ridiculous Munro altitude again. It would be such a pleasure to write to the SMC suggesting a demotion. Just imagine the howls of rage!

Closing the Book

We considered the perfect murder:
An icicle for weapon, one to leave
No fingerprint, no betraying chemicals,
Nothing lying hidden in the scree.
Little did I think it would be used on me!

Too many Buachailles, too many Bens; you
Grow careless and imagination frosts its roots.
The fatal blizzard usually catches the climber unawares,
Avalanches are what happen to other people,
An icicle in the heart is much less dramatic:
It doesn't hit the news or even the SMC Journal list.
Nobody notices the clinkered climber ageing past
Peching on the rough track down to Lagangarbh,
Nobody sees the icicle buried in his heart
Or notices the water melting into his veins.
His smile is a grimace but it hides the pains.
I tried to pull the fatal weapon out, constantly,
But there was nothing to grip. I never saw it strike.
The Season's accelerating pages ran out.
Only the blurb's angled propaganda remains
And the colourful cover. Look well! No time for tears –
It's too late, always, so make a route of your years.

Schiehallion! Schiehallion! Schiehallion!

And what was the toast?
Schiehallion! Schiehallion! Schiehallion.
Edwin Morgan: *Canedolia*

My mother's mother came from Kinloch Rannoch so we didn't really have a 'holiday home' in the accepted sense (which we thought was only for the very rich) but rather we inherited the house. During the war and just afterwards nobody wanted to buy property in the Highlands and by then we children were old enough that it became the economic place to go for holidays. It wasn't all that big a house. It was called *Schiehallion*.

Schiehallion, the peak, dominated the village and its name translated as something like the *fairy hill of the Caledonians*. We came to regard it very much as *our* hill for, unlike most visitors and all residents, our family actually climbed it. I made my first ascent when I was seven, being the indulged youngest, which had Tom, three years older, complaining (he'd been nine when first taken) and Margaret, several years older again, acting the very grand lady towards me.

The climb took all day for we started and finished from home in Kinloch Rannoch with none of the present big carpark halfway up the hill by the Maskylene memorial and a beaten trail up the boring long east ridge. We went up from Tempar always – when we reached it, for we seemed to find interests every few yards of the four mile walk. Our parents would comment on harvest prospects or the state of the lambs, or chat to old Mrs Robertson at the gatehouse of Inverhadden, the big house, while we would seek out rabbits from the hedgerows with the dog or learnt the names of flowers and birds. On the way back we might collect mushrooms in the Bunrannoch fields or bramble along the tangly bits. Food, waterproofs and the daft things youngsters carried went in ex-WD haversacks that had our names (and some unknown's number) inked on them. They had to, to avoid mix-ups for, besides our parents and the three of us, we often had cousins (mostly the twins Joe and Janet) along too and sometimes other grown-ups or friends. I suppose the Schiehallion expeditions were always saved for good days for we always seemed to have a tremendous panorama from the top and we always seemed to spend half the day in the Tempar Burn.

No climb would have been complete without a swim. If it was roasting hot (and the middle of the summer could be very hot sometimes) we spent hours in the burn on the way up. And on the way home at the last pool everyone went in (the cottage could not cope with cleaning mobs of sweaty climbers). Starkers of course, which we thought nothing about till one summer Margaret actually arrived at the summit still naked and rather shocked a party who'd come up the other way. It was all very casual, the gaggle of kids strung out for miles, never a map or compass in sight. Later, I discovered father always had these along and he kept a wary eye on all of us, however free we felt. But it was the way to treat the hills. We all loved our Schiehallion climbs. My last count showed I've been up 37 times. Some of the others must have been up more and Margaret I know takes her children up. I just wish I could join them for, though I became the Munro-bagger of the family, I ended working abroad and visits home had to be carefully planned for new ticks on the Tables. Pity I can't swap a surplus of Schiehallions for a few remote buggers.

Not that I've been up Schiehallion for a few years now. Though I try not to think so, maybe the last visit has affected me more than I'd like to admit. Perhaps I should be heading for the peak next time I'm in Scotland. See what happens. I'd perhaps have to do it in winter then too, or late autumn, with a line of white above the 2,500-level (or do Brits think metric now?) for that was how it was last time. That time.

Rannochside in late autumn! Can anything beat it with the golden birch trees set in a world of dark greens and fire-touched colours? It was just that which I'm sure lured me back. I'll swear the hired car swung up the hill at Trinafour of its own accord. I'd every intention of heading up Glen Lyon (also very lovely) for Stuchd an Lochain and/or Meall Buidhe, instead there I was twisting up the old, familiar way, then turning off at Loch Kinardochy to pass the Braes farm and down by the little reedy lochan. I parked by the Tempar Burn bridge.

People sometimes say 'How can you keep on going up a hill by the same way? Isn't it boring?' Of course it isn't! Especially with Schiehallion, *our* Schiehallion. Every yard seemed to bring back memories. Such as 'Tom's cairn' (our private name, recalling where my big brother on one occasion suddenly stopped his talkative ascent and spewed his guts out for no obvious reason – nobody else was ill of the ten people on the hill that day. Down left lay 'Maggie's mire' as we'd nicknamed a green sphagnum pool. Chuntering down, Margaret had turned to warn the rest of us, 'Be careful now. There's a horrible pool somewhere here' – and turned to go straight into it up to her tits. We killed ourselves laughing.

The wintry sun glittered on the pools up Gleann Mor that moats Schiehallion to the south, a green glen as there is a band of limestone. What days we had exploring its length with pools, caves, a bothy for some rare nights out. As I climbed on, the whole length of Loch Rannoch lay a-glitter, a highway leading the eye away out over the great moor to the far guardian peaks of Glen Etive and Glen Coe. I hadn't realised how much I loved that bit of county till then. There was Creag a' Bharr too, under the witches' hill, Beinn a' Chuallaich. How often we'd followed the Allt Mor waterslide out of the village up to the schisty rocks where big cousins introduced us to rock-climbing. Starting in the centre of Scotland, how could you *not* become a Munro-bagger I used to ask. Wasn't this, too, the parish of Rev. A. E. Robertson, the first Munroist nearly a century ago?

Schiehallion's top rocks were all covered in snow, a white sugar still in

Schiehallion from the road south above Aberfeldy

chill freshness. The well-remembered height: 3,547 ft. I reeled off names of visible friends, from Macdhui to Ben Lui, from the Lomonds to Ben Alder, rubbing hands together, partly in glee, partly because they were freezing cold! My eye was ranging over Ben Vrachie and the Beinn a' Ghlo peaks when I sensed rather than heard a footstep behind me. I turned to find another climber arriving at the trig point.

'Aye,' I greeted him.

He smiled back.

'Fantastic view in these conditions, isn't it?'

He followed my sweeping arm, the smile broadening across his face, a face at once strikingly handsome, an ageless glow of healthy living suffusing his features. He could have been anything over 30. Sixty even. Hardly talkative though.

It was too chilly to linger and I set off down the west ridge, by which we'd both come up, giving the other a nod and a grin *en passant*. He barely noticed. Or the sun dazzled him. I think he was telling off the hills of memory too, away in that golden west. I stopped several times just to gaze along the loch towards the sunset lands. Just before leaving the snow level, where the rough going over rocks had stopped and the snow lay on a kindlier surface, I noticed a set of footprints paralleling my own upward tracks. What astonished me was to see the clear marks of nails.

For goodness sake! Nails went out just after the war. A few old fogies kept on using them till they either died off, or their boots did, and nobody stocked such things any more. I hadn't seen nails for 20 years. Crampons now scratched rock, not nails. I chortled over this as I brushed through the heather down to the stile and the row of oaks back to the bridge. It was only on the boring drive along the A9 to Stirling that I began to recall other details of our encounter.

The man's face had been so lively and attractive that I'd barely looked him over but what came back was strange. He had been wearing a tie. And tweeds. OK, plenty of keepers wear tweeds but not cut like that. It was a gentleman's suit, from God knows what vintage, a grey-green with a gentle check of heather brown. Damn! Why hadn't I looked at his footwear? Why hadn't I *really* looked at him? But why should I have? He was just another climber enjoying the sparkling autumn afternoon on one of the best of Munros. We don't barge in on each other in such circumstances. Was his hair fair or greying? I couldn't recall even that and I'd certainly looked him in the face. I'd know the face anywhere. Pity I wasn't heading for Kinloch. The locals at the 'Bun' might have answered some of my questions about the antiquely equipped bloke. I switched on the radio and let the matter drift out of my mind. Back to Tom's house at Kirki.

But things kept coming back over the next few weeks. I left Scotland with a useful 22 new Munros from the fortnight's holiday (only 17 to go!), had a week in the head office in London and was soon sweating it out in the Gulf once more.

One of my treasured possessions is a complete set of the Scottish Mountaineering Club *Journal*. (*Munro's Tables* appeared first of all in an 1891 number.) Though I wasn't a great climber I'd been elected to the club a decade ago and picked up early bound volumes from a club sale. Others came in dribs and drabs from dealers and bookshops. A bit extravagant but I didn't have many extravagances so felt over the moon when the last missing numbers turned up and I could get them all bound properly – bound in buckram I'm afraid. Only the first ten volumes were already beautifully bound in leather and the dry heat means they leave a dust on my hands whenever I look at them. I don't very often. Too busy.

However, a local holiday gave me a free evening and, after I'd written a couple of dutiful letters, I pulled out a few early volumes of the SMCJ. It was always amusing to compare their accounts of days over Munros I'd done recently. Like Sir Hugh having the ice scraped off his back after a tussle on the hills above the A9. Heavens! He tackled such in tweeds – or kilt – and the big hobnailers of the club song.

Nails! In a flash the figure I'd met on top of Schiehallion was smiling at me. In the mind's eye. He'd been dressed in that sort of garb. Had the snow been old and icy he'd have an ice axe five feet long! I was letting my mind go wild.

But . . . But . . .

'But me no buts.' I tried to shake the picture away . . . went and poured a surreptitious G & T . . . took journals and drink out on to the verandah. A pattern of railings fell on the page as the low sun spread shadows that would bring a blessed coolness to the day. Soon I was carried away to the Highlands as I dipped and browsed through those dusty tomes.

I'd carried out three volumes and, when I opened the last at random, it was at an obituary portrait. Before it could register, the phone rang and I got snarled up in the business that was not supposed to follow me home from the office. After several calls I ordered supper and ate it in rather distracted fashion, my mind half on what had cropped up (the telephone call) and half on I knew not what connected with what I was doing earlier – whatever that was. Something to do with the SMC journals.

Abd el Ali had carried them in when drawing the curtains. He carried my glass off with a grimace. So I went through the motions again (in my imagination), reconstructing the scene to try and jog the memory. Took out a G & T. Opened the journals. I recalled most of the hills or stories I'd read. Not senile yet anyway. I'd only just opened the third journal when the phone rang. There was something about a picture in it. I'd only just glanced at it when the bloody phone rang. Then I saw the picture again, in my mind, and the hair on my neck rose like a cat's. Literally. The face in the obituary photograph of 1909 had been the same as the face I had seen on top of Schiehallion in 1979.